A
STRAIGHTFORWARD GUIDE TO
COMMONHOLDERS' AND
LEASEHOLDERS' RIGHTS

Third Edition

JOHN BRYANT
STRAIGHTFORWARD PUBLISHING
www.straightforwardco.co.uk

Straightforward Publishing
61 Inniskilling Road
London E13 9LD

British Library Cataloguing in publication data. A Catalogue record for this book is available from the British Library.

ISBN 19031909 18 X

Cover design by Straightforward Graphics

Printed by Bookcraft, Wiltshire.

A Straightforward Guide to
COMMONHOLDERS AND LEASEHOLDERS RIGHTS

INTRODUCTION

INTRODUCTION

The recent passage of the Commonhold and Leasehold Reform Act 2002 has refocused attention on the complex, and sometimes troubled, issue of the ownership of flats. The Act has made further changes to the law of landlord and tenant as it affects freeholders and leaseholders, and it has also introduced an entirely new type of tenure, called 'commonhold', specifically intended for blocks of flats.

However, traditional leasehold ownership will continue to dominate flat ownership for many years to come, and this dominance is reflected in this book. It deals chiefly with flats, since leasehold ownership of houses is now rare for reasons explained in Chapter Four. Its aim is to alert current and potential future leaseholders to the problems involved in owning a lease, and to warn them what to look out for. It is not, however, a substitute for proper independent legal advice. This is because leases vary enormously, so that a book of this kind cannot do more than look at them in general terms. At several points in the text leaseholders, and intending leaseholders, are advised to consult a solicitor, and the opportunity is taken to repeat this warning here. It is hoped, however, that this book will help people make sense more easily of what a solicitor may say.

The widespread use of leasehold is essentially a contrivance: it is an attempt to overcome a legal obstacle. The obstacle is that English property law thinks wholly in terms of land, whereas ordinary people, especially when they are trying to buy a place to live, think in terms of buildings. The typical buyer probably thinks he has bought a house, while the law insists that, in fact, he has bought a plot of land - the fact that a house happens to stand on it is almost beside the point as far as legal theory is concerned. But the law's peculiar way of looking at things does not make much practical difference when it comes to houses: the difficulty lies with flats.

How can it be possible to buy a flat when there is no specific bit of land on which the flat can uniquely be described as standing? The law's devotion to the idea of land makes ownership of a flat, strictly speaking, an impossibility: what flat 'owners' have actually bought is not the flat itself but the right to occupy and use it. This right is embodied in a formal agreement, called a lease, with the owner of the land.

Because the book necessarily focuses on problems and contentious areas, some readers may interpret it as a coded warning not to get involved in leasehold ownership at all. This is not intended. About three quarters of a million people in England and Wales own residential leases, and the great majority of them have no reason to regret it: the author himself is a very satisfied leaseholder. Moreover, leasehold, as mentioned above and explained more fully in Chapter One, is usually the only option for anyone that wants to buy a home but does not want, or cannot afford, a house.

A final note: this book is written by a non-lawyer and it is, emphatically, intended for the non-lawyer. Every effort has been made throughout to avoid legal terminology and to explain things in as straightforward a way as possible. However, some of the key legal points involved are unavoidably complex, so the book is a compromise between the need to be clear and accessible and the need to be comprehensive and reliable. It is hoped that the compromise that has been struck is a fair one: but any comments or criticisms will be very gratefully received. They should be sent to Straightforward Publishing, 61 Inniskilling Road, London E13 9LD.

John Bryant
1st January 2003

COMMONHOLD AND LEASEHOLD

Commonhold and Leasehold Reform Act 2002

The Commonhold and Leasehold Reform Act 2002 introduces into English law an entirely new form of tenure, namely commonhold. It is specifically targeted at blocks of flats, where leasehold has been the normal form of tenure until now.

The Government hopes that commonhold will avoid the tensions and conflicts that have sometimes arisen between leaseholders and freeholders. Time will tell whether that hope will be realised. If it is, doubtless commonhold will come to supersede leasehold as the normal form of tenure for premises divided into flats. For the present, however, commonhold and leasehold regimes will operate side by side, with leasehold predominating.

But it would be very reasonable for a flat owner to say at this point, "Wait a minute. Commonhold has been brought in as an alternative to leasehold; but what was wrong with leasehold? And why do I have to trouble myself with all this anyway? Why can't I simply own my flat, the same way as other people own their houses?"

This is a very fair question. To answer it, we need to look at how the law regards property ownership.

Freehold and Leasehold

The law does not look at property in the same way as most lay people. Most people think in terms of houses and other buildings; the law is more interested in the land beneath. A freehold home owner will say "I own my house." But the law will say "He owns the land on which is built the house he lives in." To the law, the key point is that he owns the land - the buildings on it are incidental.

For practical purposes, the strongest form of title to land is that of freeholder. Freehold title lasts for ever; it may be bought and sold, or passed by inheritance. In short, freehold title is tantamount to outright ownership, and is taken as such for the purposes of this book.

Freeholders may, of course, use their land for their own purposes. The freehold home owner is merely the most familiar example. But they may also, if they wish, allow other people to use their land. And this is where leases, and other forms of tenure, come in.

Suppose you would like to make use of a piece of land owned by someone else. The owner is unwilling to sell it to you, but, having no immediate use for it himself, is willing to allow you to use it for a time, perhaps in exchange for payment. At its simplest, this arrangement implies no more than a licence - the owner's (i.e. landlord's) permission for you to be on his land.

But such a licence can be revoked by the landlord at any time, with or without a good reason. As such it is not very valuable, so if the owner wants to make money by allowing other people to use his land, he needs to give them a legal status that they will be willing to pay for. This is achieved by granting a lease or tenancy. It should be noted here that, from the legal point of view, a lease and a tenancy are the same thing; but in practice, the terms tend to be used in different contexts. This is explained below: for the present, we shall call it a lease.

A lease grants the leaseholder permission to use the land for a certain period, which can be anything from a day or two to several thousand years. It will usually attach conditions, for example that the leaseholder must pay rent (usually a sum of money, although in principle other goods or services could constitute rent). The lease may, but does not have to, put certain restrictions on what the leaseholder may do with the land. But it must, in order to be a lease rather than merely a licence, grant the leaseholder 'exclusive possession'. This is the right to exclude other people, especially the landlord, from the land. Such a right need not be absolute, and exceptions to it are explained later in the book: but it is enough to give the leaseholder a high degree of control over the land, which has become, for the duration of the lease, very much the leaseholder's land rather than the freeholder's. A lease, unless it contains a stipulation to the contrary, may be bought, sold, or inherited; if this happens, all the rights and duties under it pass to the new owner.

Leases and Tenancies

Confusion is often caused by the fact that, although the terms leaseholder (or lessee) and tenant are legally interchangeable, they tend to be used in different senses. The tendency is to refer to short leases as tenancies: the more substantial the rights conferred, and the longer the period for which they run, the likelier it is that the agreement will be referred to as a lease. For the purposes of this book, an agreement will be referred to as a 'tenancy' if it is periodic or runs for a fixed term of less than seven years. A fixed term agreement running for more than seven years will be referred to as a 'lease'.

A 'periodic' tenancy is one that runs from period to period (usually, from week to week or month to month) until something intervenes to stop it, and is conditional on payment of rent. A tenancy that runs for a fixed term of less than seven years has a definite date of expiry but is otherwise similar to a periodic tenancy and will depend on regular payment of rent. Tenancies granted by local authorities and housing associations tend to be periodic; private landlords generally grant either periodic tenancies or short fixed-term tenancies (typically, six months). At any rate, the landlord of a periodic or short-term tenancy will usually accept most of the responsibility for maintaining the property and will charge a relatively high rent to allow for this. If the tenancy is for residential property, the landlord's duty to maintain the dwelling is imposed by law (Landlord and Tenant Act 1985).

It is common for private landlords to insist on prepayment of rent or a deposit before granting a tenancy, and many landlords will levy a separate service charge to cover the cost of some activities that are peripheral to the central one of providing housing; but despite these costs it would be true to say that the principal financial responsibility accepted by a periodic or short-term tenant is that of paying the rent.

The position of a leaseholder is very different. The major financial commitment will usually be a substantial initial payment either to the landlord (if the lease is newly created) or to the previous leaseholder. There is still a rent, called a ground rent, payable to the landlord, but it is usually a notional amount (£50 or £100 a year is not uncommon). Its purpose is not so much to give the landlord an income as to give the leaseholder an annual reminder that ultimate ownership of the land is not his.

Types of Leasehold Property

In the context of residential property, it should be noted that the great majority of leases relate to flats rather than houses. This is because of the legal concept of land tenure as described above. If a builder buys some freehold land and covers it in houses, it is possible to parcel out the area so that each bit of freehold land, and

12

the house standing on it, can be sold separately. It does not matter if the houses are semi-detached or terraced, because there is well-established law governing party walls of adjoining freeholders. But if there are flats, the builder has a problem: how can the flats be sold since they cannot be said to stand on separate and distinct bits of land? The answer is to sell leases.

Where flats are sold, each purchaser acquires a lease that gives him specified rights over the parcel of land on which the flats stand. These rights, of course, are shared by the leaseholders of the other flats. In addition, however, each leaseholder gains the right to exclusive possession of part of the building occupying the land - his own flat. The leaseholder would say "I own my flat", but the law says "He owns a lease granting him certain rights, in particular that of access, to a defined parcel of land and the right of exclusive possession of specified parts of a building erected on that land." This may seem a slightly unusual way of looking at it, but it is fundamental to understanding the way that the law sees the relationship between leaseholders of flats and their freeholders.

The freehold of flatted property will often be retained by the developer, although sometimes it will be sold to a property company. Formerly, it was common practice for the freehold to be retained even when separate houses were built. This allowed the freeholder to retain an interest in the property and, above all, to regain full possession of it when the lease expired. However, the position of freeholders has been weakened by three key pieces of legislation, the Leasehold Reform Act 1967, the Leasehold Reform, Housing and Urban Development Act 1993, and the Commonhold and Leasehold Reform Act 2002. These Acts are described in detail in Chapter Four: their overall effect is to entitle leaseholders either to the freehold of houses or to a new lease of flats. In view of the legislation, there is now little point in the original owner's

13

attempting to retain the freehold of land on which houses have been built. The exception is where a house is sold on the basis of shared ownership - see below.

Most residential leasehold property therefore consists of flats. Of these, most are in the private sector, comprising purpose-built blocks and (especially in London) conversions of what were once large single houses. The freehold will usually belong to the developer, to a property company, or sometimes to the original owner of the site.

House leases normally give most of the repairing responsibility to the leaseholder - services provided by the freeholder, and therefore service charges, are minimal. In flats, however, although the leaseholder will normally be responsible for the interior of the flat, the freeholder will maintain the fabric of the building and will recoup the costs of doing so by levying service charges on the leaseholders. This is an area of such potential conflict between leaseholders and freeholders that it has been the subject of legislation. It is dealt with fully in Chapter Three.

Mixed-tenure blocks: the right to buy
The general shift from renting to owning means that sometimes flats have been sold in blocks that were originally developed for letting to tenants: the result is often a 'mixed-tenure' block, with both leaseholders and tenants. Although this sometimes happens in the private sector, it is particularly common in blocks owned by local authorities and housing associations, for it is to these that the statutory right to buy applies. This right was created by the Housing Act 1980 and allows most local authority tenants, and some housing association tenants, to buy their homes at a heavily discounted price. Tenants of houses are normally sold the freehold, but tenants of flats become leaseholders.

The right to buy, often seen as the flagship policy of Margaret Thatcher's government, was bitterly opposed, because of the loss it involves of homes otherwise available for letting to the needy and because its popularity with council tenants called into question their previously solid electoral support for Labour. On both counts, its critics' fears have to some extent been realised; however, the right to buy has become an increasingly accepted feature of local authority housing. More recently, a similar but less generous scheme has been introduced covering many housing association tenants not already qualifying for the full right to buy.

Purchasing a council home has been, for most of the million or so that have done so, a very satisfactory investment. A minority of purchasers have, however, met with serious difficulties, particularly where they have become leaseholders in mixed tenure blocks of flats: Chapter Three looks at some of the problems affecting management and service charges.

Shared ownership
Another result of the trend towards home ownership has been the dramatic expansion of shared ownership. This is a form of tenure that combines leasing and renting. However, the term 'shared ownership' is something of a misnomer because ownership is not, in fact, shared between the leaseholder and the freeholder. The lease relates to the whole property, not part of it, and the shared owner is as entitled as any other leaseholder to consider himself the owner of his house. The key point about shared ownership leases is not that they give an inferior form of tenure to other leases but that they have different conditions attached. The leaseholder pays less than the full value of the lease; typically, half. In exchange for this concession, he pays not the normal notional ground rent but a much more substantial rent. However, he is much more a leaseholder than he is a tenant, and, like other leaseholders (but

15

unlike tenants) is responsible for the internal repair of the property and, in the case of houses, usually the fabric of the building too.

Shared owners usually have the right to increase their stake as and when they can afford it: this is called 'staircasing' because the owner's share goes up in steps. If the property is a house, the freehold will normally be transferred when the owner's share reaches 100%, and he will then be in the same position as any other freehold home owner. If it is a flat, he will continue to be a leaseholder but there will no longer be a rental (other than ground rent).

Head Leases and Subleases

For the sake of clarity and brevity, this book has been written throughout on the basis that there are only two parties involved: the freeholder and the leaseholder. Usually this picture is accurate; but it is the right of the leaseholder, unless the lease specifically forbids it, to sublet the property, or part of it, to someone else. This means that the leaseholder delegates some of his rights over the property to another person. Obviously, he cannot delegate rights greater than his own, so that if he holds a lease of the property running until 2025 he cannot grant a sublease running until 2050. And he cannot grant a sublease of the whole of his rights because this would leave him with no interest in the property: it would, in fact, amount to the same as an assignment (see Chapter Two). So it is necessary for a sublease that the original leaseholder be left with something; either some period of time or some part of the property.

It is possible in theory to have a whole hierarchy of leases applying to a particular property, starting with the freehold, then the head lease, then a sublease, followed by sub-subleases and possibly sub-sub-subleases below those. There are two rules that limit this kind of proliferation: one, explained above, is that each lease must confer less, in space or time or both, than the one above it; and the other, that if a lease may not be held by the same person as hold the lease (or freehold) immediately above it.

Even with these limitations, however, long chains of ownership can develop. Suppose I own the freehold of a certain piece of land. I am unwilling to sell it outright but I agree to lease it for 125 years to a property developer to build flats, so he becomes the head leaseholder and leases the flats for 99 years to individual subleaseholders. One of these leases his flat for 25 years to someone that, in turn, lets it on a tenancy. The tenant then sublets to some other person who (remembering that tenancies and leases are legally the same) thus becomes a sub-sub-sub-subleaseholder (if I have counted correctly). And it is possible to devise even taller hierarchies of lease than this, provided always that no one holds a lease from himself and that each lease grants less, even if only slightly, than the one above it.

Commonhold

To try to deal with problems arising from the relationship between freeholders and leaseholders, a new form of tenure, 'commonhold', was created by the Commonhold and Leasehold Reform Act 2002. It is designed specifically for use in blocks of flats, and the idea is that all the individual flat owners (or 'unit holders', as the Act calls them) will belong to a 'commonhold association', a registered company that operate under a constitution (the 'memorandum and articles') and act in accordance with a 'commonhold community statement'.

This arrangement ensures that each unit holder will have two separate interests in relation to the property: individually, in his own particular unit, and collectively, in the block as a whole. The relevant parts of the 2002 Act will not be implemented until

17

October 2003 at the earliest, and even after that it will take some time for new commonhold developments to start operating, so it will be some years before commonhold will really be put to the test. Meanwhile, the Government is consulting about detailed regulations for commonhold, including the standard constitution (memorandum and articles) for commonhold associations, and the standard form for commonhold community statements. At the time of writing it seems likely that these standard documents will be very detailed and specific.

The standard forms include some welcome recognition that disputes will inevitably occur within commonhold schemes, and disputes will be referred to an ombudsman, but it still seems likely that the commonhold association will be struggling to find an effective remedy when individual unit holders default on their obligations. This remains a major concern about the future effectiveness of the commonhold system.

Once the relevant parts of the 2002 Act are brought into effect, in October 2003 or later, it will be possible to register newly developed blocks as commonhold, but it will be virtually impossible to convert existing blocks to commonhold because the 2002 Act requires unanimous consent, something that is unlikely to be achieved. Therefore, unless the rules are changed again it seems that leasehold will remain the dominant form of tenure for flats for many years to come. However, reasons are given in the last Chapter for believing that commonhold is unlikely to result in the benefits its promoters have claimed for it.

-2-

OBLIGATIONS OF FREEHOLDER AND LEASEHOLDER

General Principles

For centuries the law did little to regulate the relationship between freeholders and leaseholders. The view was taken that they had entered into the relationship of their own free will, and it was up to them to agree whatever terms and conditions they liked. If either party did not keep the bargain, he could of course be sued in the courts, but, on the whole, the law did not interfere in the bargain itself.

In the twentieth century, however, the view grew up that some types of bargain are inherently unfair and even those that are not might still be open to exploitation.

An example of the first type is an agreement that residential property will revert to the original freeholder at the end of a long lease. This meant that when 99 year leases expired, leaseholders found that their homes had abruptly returned to the outright ownership of the heir of the original freeholder, leaving them as mere trespassers liable to be ejected at any time. In practice, freeholders were usually willing to grant a fresh lease, but sometimes only at a very high price that the leaseholder might well be unable to afford. In some cases, freeholders insisted on reclaiming the property however much the leaseholder offered, and the law supported them. This is the state of affairs that led to legislation entitling almost all residential leaseholders to extend their leases, and many of them to claim the freehold. This is dealt with in Chapter Four.

The freeholder's right to demand a service charge is an example of an arrangement that is fair in principle but open to abuse in practice. It is inevitable, especially in flats, that responsibility for some types of repair cannot be ascribed to any individual leaseholder and must therefore be retained by the freeholder; who must, in turn, recoup the cost from leaseholders. However, some freeholders abused this system by levying extravagant service charges that made the service charge a source of profit. To prevent this, there is now a substantial body of legislation designed to ensure that freeholders carry out only the works that are really necessary and that they recover their legitimate costs and no more. The complicated rules governing this are chiefly found in the Landlord and Tenant Act 1985 (as amended) and are described in Chapter Three.

Under the Landlord and Tenant Act 1987, either party to a long lease (one originally granted for at least 21 years) may go to the Leasehold Valuation Tribunal (or 'LVT') to argue that the lease is deficient in some way and needs to be changed. If only the one lease is affected, the tribunal may vary it. Sometimes, however, a number of leases may need to be changed; in this case either the freeholder or 75% of the leaseholders may apply.

Obligations of Leaseholders
The obligations of leaseholders are set out in the lease; indeed, since it is a document drafted by or on behalf of freeholders, one of its main aims is to tell leaseholders what they must and must not do. However, legislation and judicial decisions sometimes come to the leaseholder's assistance.

Consumer legislation can also apply to leases; in particular, the Unfair Terms in Consumer Contracts Regulations 1999 (which replace earlier regulations made in 1995) have a major impact.

These apply to standard terms in contracts. This means they normally cover the terms of leases, which are usually presented to potential leaseholders as a package with no opportunity to renegotiate individual terms. Occasionally, however, individual terms can be specifically negotiated and it should be noted that in that case the Unfair Terms Regulations do not apply. Nor will they apply to any lease granted before the earlier version of the regulations came in in July 1995.

The Office of Fair Trading has issued advice about the types of term that are likely to be judged unfair in the context of assured tenancies. The OFT has not issued advice about long leases, but it is likely that similar standards would apply.

a: Plain and intelligible language
Over many years property lawyers have developed an obscure and technical language that can have the effect of excluding outsiders. This form of 'legalese' is characterised by unwieldy sentences with few (or no) commas to break them up, long lists often consisting of different names for the same thing, and a vocabulary of unfamiliar words and (worst of all) familiar words given unfamiliar meetings.

For instance, in normal English the verb 'determine' means 'ascertain' or 'firmly decide', but when a property lawyer applies it to a lease it means 'end' or 'terminate' (as in 'the lease shall determine if...'). Property lawyers also have a well-merited reputation for using words like 'hereinafter' and 'aforesaid', which, although not ambiguous, are hardly everyday English, while occasional outbreaks of Latin are not unknown (*pari passu* and *mutatis mutandis*).

Thankfully, this style is going out of fashion and an increasing number of modern leases are being written in more intelligible language, and for leases made since 1995 the Unfair Terms

21

Regulations mean that arcanely written terms may be unenforceable. However, a huge number of leases written in traditional style still have decades or even centuries to run, so unfortunately property lawyers' English will be with us for a long time yet.

b: Terms Unfair on Consumers

There are some terms to which the Office of Fair Trading objects in any consumer contract. These are terms that place an unreasonable burden on the customer (the leaseholder) or give an unfair advantage to the supplier (the freeholder). Some of these terms are common in long leases.

There may be a clause in which the leaseholder declares that he has 'read and understood' the lease, even though the document is long and complex and it unlikely that anyone would read (or understand) the whole of it. The aim is to put the leaseholder at a disadvantage in any dispute by arguing that he was fully aware of all the terms of the lease. Another way of loading the scales is a clause allowing the freeholder the final decision about vital matters, such as whether or not the freeholder and the leaseholder have fulfilled their respective obligations under the lease.

These clauses are probably unenforceable in leases made since July 1995, but in earlier leases they are probably valid.

There are other types of clause that are potentially a problem for the leaseholder. An example is a clause laying down procedural formalities. Such a clause is not necessarily a problem: for instance, leases commonly require formal communications between the freeholder and the leaseholder to be in writing, and this is a perfectly reasonable requirement because it reduces the chances misunderstandings or disputes about who said what. But it is harder to justify a requirement for notices to be sent by registered post,

22

and some leases stipulate procedures that are so onerous that the aim seems to be to deter leaseholders from exercising their rights.

Similar comments apply to clauses imposing financial penalties for breaches of the lease. This is not necessarily unreasonable, but sometimes the penalties are out of all proportion to the nature of the breach.

Some leases require the leaseholder to join with the freeholder (and help with the cost) in responding to legal or other notices pertaining to the property. Again, this may be reasonable in some circumstances, but as a blanket requirement it can act against leaseholders' interests.

An interesting and debatable issue is the prohibition of set-off, which is a standard clause in most leases. 'Set-off' is the practice of deducting (or 'setting off') from any payment made by one party under an agreement any sums that are owed by the other party. For instance, suppose a leaseholder considers that a repair to the fabric of the building is the freeholder's responsibility, but the freeholder either disputes this or fails to take any action. Eventually the leaseholder does the work at his own expense, and next time the annual service charge falls due he reimburses himself by deducting, or 'setting off', the cost from his service charge payment.

Leaseholders like set-off because it is an easy way of reclaiming disputed sums from the freeholder, and it shifts onto the freeholder the onus of continuing the dispute. Freeholders dislike it for exactly the same reasons, which is why leases normally prohibit it. The Office of Fair Trading, in its advice on assured tenancies, says that prohibiting set-off is unfair, but it is not clear whether the same advice would apply to leases.

The possibility that unfair, or potentially unfair, clauses will feature in a lease underlines the need for competent legal advice before signing it. An experienced solicitor will be able to advise whether doubtful clauses can be, or are likely to be, used against leaseholders. Leaseholders may also have remedies available under the Landlord and Tenant Act: this is covered below and, in the key area of service charges, in the next Chapter.

c: Restrictive clauses in leases

So far, we have looked at leases as if they were consumer contracts, and outlined some of the clauses they may contain that could affect leaseholders in their capacity as consumers. But there are some further potentially difficult terms that relate specifically to property issues. These terms are not necessarily unreasonable. For example, in a lease concerning an upstairs flat it would be quite normal to have a clause requiring the leaseholder to keep the premises carpeted. This makes sense because bare floors, although currently very fashionable, could be very noisy for the people in the flat below.

The Office of Fair Trading's advice identifies several types of sweeping provisions that would, if they were enforced, considerably restrict the tenant's ability to live a normal life. Although the OFT's advice relates to assured tenancies, similar objections would probably apply to these clauses in leases. For example:

- **Pets** Leases often lay down that the leaseholder may not own pets, or may not do so without the freeholder's permission.

- **Upkeep** Leases may say that the leaseholder must decorate periodically - say, every five or seven years. Where there is a garden, it is common for the leaseholder to be required to keep it in good order.

24

- **Business** Leases often lay down that the leaseholder must not run any sort of business from his home.

- **Use as residence** A lease will generally say that the property is to be used for the residential purposes of the leaseholder and his household, and that it cannot be sublet. It will sometimes attempt to restrict how many people may live there apart from the leaseholder.

- **Other** Leases sometimes forbid such things as the keeping of flammable materials and the installation of television aerials or satellite dishes. They may require leaseholders to drain hot water systems whenever they are away, or keep the premises clean and free of dust.

It is easy to see why freeholders want such clauses in the lease: it is because they realise that there will be serious problems if someone attempts, for instance, to keep four alsatians in a studio flat. The neighbours will be inconvenienced and will complain to the freeholder, and leases of other flats in the same block will become difficult to sell.

The same arguments could apply if one of the leaseholders allows his flat to fall into complete decorative decay or if he runs a noisy and busy trade from his home.

But the kind of blanket rules that appear in many leases go too far. A rule against any pets at all forbids not only four noisy alsatians but also entirely inoffensive pets such as a budgie or a goldfish. In the same way, prohibiting business activities means that the leaseholder may not use his home to write a book for publication, or address envelopes, and so on - types of homeworking that could not possibly inconvenience anyone.

The rule against sub-letting also prevents leaseholders from exploiting the value of their property by letting it out, something that is open to most home-owners and is increasingly accepted as normal.

For leases made since July 1995, these sweeping clauses are probably unfair and unenforceable. But even for older leases, the reality is that such broad provisions are seldom enforced. Freeholders, and their lawyers, like them because they feel that they preserve their freedom of action, allowing them to decide whether or not to enforce the lease if it is clear that one of these blanket conditions is being broken. But there are two problems with this attitude.

The first is that it creates uncertainty in the minds of leaseholders. Suppose the leases in a block of flats prohibit all pets, but leaseholder A has a goldfish and no action has been taken even though the freeholder is aware of the infringement. Leaseholder B may well conclude that there will be no objection if he gets a cat. If still there is no action, leaseholder C may feel able to get a couple of dogs - and so on. So the fact that restrictions are so broad can have the paradoxical effect of reducing their effectiveness.

The second problem is that if, in the example just given, the freeholder takes legal action to force C to get rid of the dogs, it is possible that C will argue in court that the treatment of the other leaseholders shows that the freeholder is not seriously interested in banning pets and that the action has been motivated rather by petty spite or bias.

It would be better if freeholders and their lawyers drafted leases that say what they mean: not that leaseholders may have no pets at all, but that they may have no pets apt to damage the property or cause inconvenience or annoyance to other persons. The same principle should apply to clauses dealing with sub-letting or working from home.

It is unfortunate that this book is forced to advise leaseholders to ignore some parts of their leases. The responsibility for this, however, lies with freeholders and their lawyers for writing into standard leases blanket conditions purporting to prohibit entirely inoffensive behaviour. This practice makes it inevitable, in the real world, that leaseholders will disregard certain clauses, and that books like this will have to give them some indication of when they can probably do so safely. Most leaseholders exercise common sense and realise that the freeholder is unlikely to take action unless there is a complaint, which means that the leaseholder may do almost whatever he pleases provided he refrains from provoking anyone. It is sensible to stay on good terms with neighbours to ensure that if anything is bothering them they take it up directly with you rather than report the matter to the freeholder. Other leaseholders will also be able to tell you what view has been taken in the past - both by other residents and by the freeholder - in doubtful cases.

d: Restrictions on sale

Some leases restrict the kind of person to whom the lease may be sold (or 'assigned' - see below). For example, a housing scheme may have been intended specifically for the elderly. Clearly, it will not be maintained as such if leaseholders are free to assign or bequeath their leases to whomever they please, so the lease will say that it may be assigned only to persons above a certain age, and that if it is inherited by anyone outside the age group it must be sold on to someone qualified to hold it. Although this could be described as an onerous term because it makes it more difficult to find a buyer and may reduce the lease's value, it is reasonable given the need to ensure that the scheme continues to house elderly people exclusively. And the restriction it imposes is not too severe because so many potential purchasers qualify.

However, some leases define much more narrowly to whom they may be sold. Sometimes the freeholder is a body owned and run by the leaseholders themselves, and in these cases it is usual to require that all leaseholders must join the organisation and, if they leave it, must immediately dispose of the lease to someone that is willing to join. Again, such a term is not necessarily unacceptable. If the organisation makes relatively light demands on its members (perhaps no more than a modest admission fee or annual subscription), the restriction is unlikely greatly to diminish the value of the lease. If, however, the organisation expects much more from its members - perhaps that they actively take part in running it, or that they pay a large annual subscription - the value of the lease will be severely reduced because it will be difficult to find purchasers willing to accept the conditions. A key point is whether the organisation has power to expel members, thus forcing them to sell; and, if so, in what circumstances and by whom this power can be exercised.

e: Access
Virtually any lease will contain a clause allowing the freeholder to enter the property in order to inspect or repair it. This has the effect of qualifying the leaseholder's right of exclusive possession (see below), but only subject to certain conditions. The freeholder (or the freeholder's servants, such as agents or contractors) may enter only at reasonable times, and subject to the giving of reasonable notice. If these conditions are not met, the leaseholder is under no obligation to allow them in; and, even when the conditions are met, the landlord will be trespassing if he enters the property without the leaseholder's consent. If the leaseholder refuses consent even

though the time is reasonable and reasonable notice has been given, the landlord's remedy is to get a court order against the leaseholder compelling him to grant entry. It is probable, in such a case, that the landlord will seek, and get, an award of legal costs against the leaseholder.

f: Arbitration

Many leases contain clauses providing that disputes can be submitted to arbitration at the request of either party. By the Commonhold and Leasehold Reform Act, the effect of these clauses is limited, because the results will not be binding so far as the Leasehold Valuation Tribunal is concerned. If, however, once a dispute has arisen, the parties to agree to submit it to an agreed arbitrator, they are bound by the result, which is enforceable by the courts. If such a 'post-dispute' arbitration finds that the leaseholder is in breach, this is equivalent to a finding by the LVT and will (if the other requirements are met) allow the freeholder to proceed with forfeiture. Arbitration may be a useful mechanism in some cases, and it may be cheaper and quicker than legal action, but it may be difficult to find an arbitrator in whom both parties have confidence.

Obligations of Freeholders
a: Exclusive possession and quiet enjoyment
The first and most important obligation on the freeholder, without which there would be no legal lease at all, is to respect the leaseholder's rights of 'exclusive possession' and 'quiet enjoyment'. Exclusive possession has been explained in Chapter One as the right to occupy the property and exclude others from it, especially the freeholder. Quiet enjoyment is another way of underlining the leaseholder's rights over the property: it means that the freeholder may not interfere with the leaseholder's use of the property provided that the terms of the lease are observed.

29

However, the leaseholder's right to quiet enjoyment applies only to breaches by the freeholder or the freeholder's servants such as agents or contractors. It is important to note this because the term is sometimes thought to mean that the freeholder must protect the leaseholder against any activity by anyone that interferes with his use of the property: this is not so. For example, if the freeholder carries out some activity elsewhere in the building that interferes with the leaseholder, the leaseholder's right to quiet enjoyment has been breached and he is entitled to redress unless the freeholder can show that the activity was necessary, for instance to comply with repairing obligations under the lease. But if the interference is caused by someone else, perhaps another leaseholder, the freeholder's obligation to provide quiet enjoyment has not been breached. And it is worth stressing in this connection that even if the other leaseholder is in breach of his lease, it is entirely up to the freeholder whether or not to take action: other leaseholders have no power to force the freeholder to deal with the situation.

This means that if one leaseholder is breaking his lease by holding noisy parties late at night, the other leaseholders may ask, but may not require, the freeholder to take action to enforce the lease. They may, however, take legal action directly against the offending leaseholder for nuisance.

b: The 'section 48' notice
Another important protection for leaseholders is found in section 48 of the Landlord and Tenant Act 1987. This was designed to deal with the situation in which freeholders seek to avoid their responsibilities by (to put it bluntly) doing a disappearing act. Sometimes freeholders would provide no address or telephone number or other means of contact, meaning that leaseholders were unable to hold the freeholder to his side of the agreement. Sections 47 and 48 therefore lay down that the freeholder must formally

notify the leaseholder of his name and give an address within England and Wales at which he can be contacted, and that this information must be repeated on every demand for rent or service charge. This has proved especially valuable for leaseholders where the freeholder lives abroad, or is a company based abroad. It should be noted that the address does not have to be the freeholder's home, nor, if the freeholder is a company, its registered office; often it will be the address of a solicitor or property management company, or simply an accommodation address. But the key point is that any notice, or legal writ, is validly served if sent to that address, and the freeholder is not allowed to claim that it never came to his notice.

It is not necessary for the notice required by section 48 to be given in a separate document; it is enough if the name and address is clearly given as part of some other document such as a service charge demand. But if the necessary notice is **not** given, no payment of rent, service charge, or anything else is due to the freeholder; the leaseholder may lawfully withhold it until section 48 is complied with. But leaseholders withholding payments on this ground must be careful; once the notice is given, it has retrospective effect, so that all the money due to the freeholder then becomes due immediately. Any leaseholder withholding money on the grounds that section 48 has not been complied with should, therefore, make sure that he has the money easily available so that he can pay up if he has to.

c: Good management

The freeholder is under an obligation to ensure that his management responsibilities are carried out in a proper and appropriate way. Leaseholders can challenge the freeholder in court or at the LVT if they believe they can show that they are not receiving the standard of management to which they are entitled.

31

This may be an expensive and lengthy process but it better than the alternative, sometimes resorted to by leaseholders, of withholding rent or service charge. This is risky because, whatever the shortcomings of the freeholder's management, it puts the leaseholders in breach of the conditions of their lease and, as such, demonstrably in the wrong (even if the freeholder may be in the wrong as well).

Withholding due payments is therefore not recommended unless the freeholder is so clearly at fault that arguably no payment is due - for instance, if the service being charged for has clearly not been provided at all (as opposed to being provided inadequately), or if there has been no 'section 48' notice (see above). If leaseholders choose to withhold payment, they are strongly advised to keep the money readily to hand so that they can pay up at once if the freeholder rectifies the problem; the danger otherwise is that they will be taken to court and required to pay immediately to avoid forfeiture (see below).

Powers of Leaseholders over Management

If leaseholders want a scrutiny of the standards of management of their flats, they have power under the Leasehold Reform, Housing and Urban Development Act 1993 to demand a management audit by an auditor acting on behalf of at least two-thirds of the qualifying leaseholders. Qualifying leaseholders are those with leases of residential property originally granted for 21 years or more and requiring them to contribute to the cost of services.

The purpose of the audit, the costs of which must be met by the leaseholders demanding it, is to discover whether the freeholder's duties are being carried out efficiently and effectively. The auditor is appointed by the leaseholders and must be either a qualified accountant or a qualified surveyor and must not live in the block concerned. The auditor has the right to demand papers from the freeholder and can go to court if they are not produced.

Leaseholders' Right to Manage
Leaseholders with long leases (those originally granted for 21 years or more) also have the right to take over management of their block if they wish. This applies to blocks of two or more flats (five or more if there is a resident landlord) and no substantial non-residential part. It does not apply if the freeholder is a local authority.

The leaseholders must first form a 'Right to Manage' company ('RtM' company), which is a limited company whose membership is confined to leaseholders and the freeholder. Before seeking to take over management the RtM company must advise all leaseholders of its intention and invite them to participate. Fourteen days after this invitation, and provided the RtM company includes at least half the eligible tenants (or both, if only two are eligible), it can serve a claim notice on the landlord (or on the Leasehold Valuation Tribunal, if the landlord is untraceable) giving at least four months' notice of its intention to take over the management. The landlord has a month to serve a counter-notice objecting to the claim, in which case the LVT will adjudicate. If no counter-notice is served, or if the LVT so decides, the RtM company duly takes over management.

The landlord must bring to an end as quickly as possible any existing management arrangements applying to the block. The RtM company takes over the landlord's management functions, including services, repairs, maintenance, improvements, and insurance. The landlord retains its role in respect of any flats without long leaseholders (for example, those let on assured tenancies), and continues to deal with forfeiture (for more on forfeiture see the section below 'If the lease is breached'). Essentially the RtM company steps into the landlord's shoes so far as management is concerned, and it is responsible to both the landlord and the individual leaseholders for the proper carrying out of its functions.

Many leases require the landlord's approval before certain things can be done, such as assigning the lease or sub-letting. The RtM company takes over this function from the landlord, but must consult the landlord before granting approval. If the landlord objects, the matter is referred to the LVT. It seems, however, that refusal of consent by the RtM is final and cannot be challenged by the landlord (although it might be challenged by the leaseholder in question on the ground that the relevant term of the lease is unenforceable). The RtM company has authority to enforce covenants in the lease, but not by means of forfeiture.

At first blush the power to take over management in this way may appear attractive. However, leaseholders should think very carefully before they commit themselves; there are some potential snags.

The biggest problem is one of enforcement. So long as all leaseholders are agreed about what needs to be done, and are all willing and able to meet their obligations (including that of paying for services), enforcement will not be an issue and all will be well. But if some individual leaseholders refuse to pay their share, or fail to abide by the covenants in their leases, the RtM company will have to act to enforce the leases and this may well be difficult. In the first place, any steps to enforce leases will pit neighbour against neighbour and are virtually certain to cause animosity in the block. Secondly, the powerful tool of forfeiture, or threatened forfeiture, is denied to a RtM company. Finally, the RtM company, unlike most freeholders, will not have any substantial financial resources that would allow it to pursue lengthy legal action against individual leaseholders.

There are other issues. The RtM company will depend on the voluntary efforts of its members, and experience shows that many people are not willing to put in the time and effort involved in attending meetings and carrying out essential administration. RtM companies have to operate under a special constitution laid down by the Government; the aim of this is to guarantee all leaseholders' rights to be involved, but because the constitution is a standard document applying to all cases it is likely that many leaseholders will find it clumsy and inflexible. Finally, there is the question of continuing relations with the freeholder, which will expect its interests as ultimate owner to be respected by the RtM company.

In short, leaseholders contemplating the formation of a RtM company need to be sure that they are committed not only for the immediate effort of setting it up but for the long haul of carrying out management in the future. They should also recognise that, no matter how united everyone may be to start with, sooner or later the issue of enforcement will rear its head. They should certainly get legal advice about their new responsibilities before committing themselves.

The law allows another remedy in extreme cases of mismanagement. A leaseholder can use the Landlord and Tenant Act 1987 to force the appointment of a managing agent to run the block instead of the freeholder. The leaseholder must serve a notice telling the freeholder what the problems are and warning that unless they are put right a Leasehold Valuation Tribunal will be asked to appoint a managing agent. The LVT may make such an order if it satisfied that it is 'just and convenient'; the Act mentions, as specific examples where this may apply, cases where the freeholder is in breach of obligations under the lease and cases where service charges are being levied in respect of work of a poor standard or an unnecessarily high standard. It should be noted that this procedure, although in some ways it resembles the procedures for collective enfranchisement in Chapter Five, differs from them in that it can be carried out by any individual leaseholder; it does not require the consent of a majority. Note too that the procedure is not available if the freeholder is a local authority, a registered housing association, or the Crown.

Recognised Tenants' Association

A recognised tenants' association (RTA), where there is one, has additional rights to be consulted about managing agents. The RTA can serve a notice requiring the freeholder to supply details of the managing agent and the terms of the management agreement. Recognised tenants' associations are more important, however, in connexion with service charges, so they are explained in the Chapter Three.

Leaseholders that are receiving a consistently poor or overpriced service may also wish to consider getting rid of the freeholder altogether by collective enfranchisement under the Leasehold Reform, Housing and Urban Development Act 1993 (see Chapter Four).

Assignment of Leases

One of the most important characteristics of a lease - in marked contrast to most tenancies - is that it may be bought and sold. Usually, the freeholder has no say in this: the leaseholder may sell to whom he likes for the best price he can get, provided that the purchaser agrees to be bound by the terms of the lease. It is, however, usual for the lease to lay down that the freeholder must be informed of any change of leaseholder.

What actually happens when a lease is sold is that the vendor agrees to transfer to the buyer his rights and obligations under the lease.

This is called 'assignment' of the lease. In some types of housing the freeholder has the right to intervene if an assignment is envisaged. The housing may, for instance, be reserved for a particular category of resident, such as the retired, so the freeholder is allowed to refuse consent to the assignment if the purchaser does not qualify.

It was mentioned above that the assignee takes over all the rights and responsibilities attaching to the lease. This means, for instance, that he takes responsibility for any arrears of service charge. This is why purchasers' solicitors go to such lengths to ensure that no arrears or other unusual obligations arc outstanding.

If the Lease Is Breached

If the terms of a lease are broken, the party offended against can go to court. This may be the leaseholder, for instance if the freeholder has failed to carry out a repair. But it is normally the freeholder that takes the leaseholder to court, for failure to pay ground rent or service charges or for breach of some other requirement.

It is for the court, if satisfied that the lease has been breached, to decide what to do. The normal remedy will be that the offending party must pay compensation and that the breach (if it is still continuing) must be put right. It is also likely that the loser will be obliged to pay the winner's legal costs as well as his own, a penalty often considerably more severe that the requirement to pay compensation.

A much more severe remedy open to the freeholder if the leaseholder is in breach is forfeiture of the lease. This means what it says: the lease is forfeit to the freeholder. Forfeiture is sometimes threatened by the more aggressive class of freeholder but the good news for leaseholders is that in practice courts have shown themselves loth to grant it except in very serious cases. Since the

Housing Act 1996 took effect, forfeiture for unpaid service charges has been made more difficult for freeholders; this is covered in the next Chapter.

Where forfeiture is threatened for any reason other than failure to pay rent (which, depending on the terms of the lease, may or may not include the service charge element), the freeholder must first serve a 'section 146 notice', so called after the relevant provision of the Law of Property Act 1925. In this he must state the nature of the breach of the lease, what action is required to put it right; if he wants monetary compensation for the breach, the notice must state this too.

Before the section 146 notice can be issued, it must be established that a breach of the lease has occurred. If the leaseholder has admitted the breach, the notice can be issued; otherwise, it must have been decided by a court, the LVT, or an independent arbitrator that the leaseholder is in breach. Moreover, the breach of the lease specified in the section 146 notice must have occurred during the twelve years preceding the notice. For breaches older than this, no valid section 146 notice can be served and so forfeiture is not available. If the notice is not complied with, the freeholder may proceed to forfeit; but the leaseholder may go to court for relief from forfeiture. In practice, courts have generally been willing to grant relief, but they cannot do so unless it is formally applied for. If the leaseholder, perhaps failing to realise the seriousness of the situation, fails to go to court and seek relief, the forfeiture will go ahead.

Forfeiture will be considered again in the next Chapter, which covers the special rules applying to forfeiture for failure to pay service charges.

The Government has announced that ultimately it intends to replace forfeiture by a different remedy that will recognise the value of the leaseholder's interest. Until this happens, however, forfeiture remains available and leaseholders must take care to avoid any possibility of its being used against them.

If the freeholder breaches the lease, the leaseholder can go to court and seek an order requiring the freeholder to remedy the breach, to pay damages, or to do both. The commonest type of breach complained of by leaseholders is failure to carry out repairs, and this explains why action by leaseholders is less usual; they know that if they force the freeholder to do repairs the costs will be recovered through service charges. Legal action may be the best course if the dispute affects a single leaseholder; but if a number of leaseholders are involved they may well prefer to get rid of the freeholder altogether by collectively enfranchising their leases as described in Chapter Four.

Leasehold Valuation Tribunals
Several references have already been made to Leasehold Valuation Tribunals. These bodies operate throughout England and Wales. They are appointed jointly by the Lord Chancellor and (in England) the Environment Secretary and (in Wales) the Welsh Secretary. They perform a large number of quasi-judicial functions in relation to property, especially leasehold property, and feature frequently in this book.

-3-

SERVICE CHARGES

The Role of Service Charges

By far the commonest cause of dispute between leaseholders and freeholders is the provision of services and, especially, the levying of service charges. In extreme cases, leaseholders have been asked to contribute thousands of pounds towards the cost of major repairs, and have even suffered forfeiture of the lease if they are unable, or unwilling, to comply. Happily, such instances are rare; but even where the service charges are more moderate, they are often resented by leaseholders. The purpose of this Chapter is to explain the legitimate purpose of service charges and the legal obligations of both the leaseholder and the freeholder, and to offer some warnings about the circumstances where very high service charges are likely to be found.

The difference between long leases and tenancies (short-term and periodic) was set out in Chapter One. One of its most important consequences is that services are paid for in a very different way. In a periodic or short-term tenancy, all the basic costs of providing and managing the housing are paid out of the rent. It is true that there will sometimes be a service charge as well, but it normally covers things such as the provision of heating or communal lighting - things that, however necessary they may be, are peripheral to the central function of providing housing. As a result, service charges in rented property are usually quite moderate and cause little argument.

Contrast the position in leasehold housing. In both types of housing, the landlord is under a legal obligation to the residents to housing, the landlord is under a legal obligation to the residents to keep the property in good condition and to carry out any work necessary for that purpose; but the landlord of rented property is expected to meet the costs from the rent, whereas the freeholder of leasehold stock has no rent to fall back on (apart from the normally negligible ground rent). How, then, are major costs to be met when they arise? The answer, of course, is from the service charge, which is, therefore, of central importance to the management of leasehold property.

From the freeholder's point of view, the logic of service charges is impeccable. It is perfectly reasonable for freeholders to point out:

*   that leaseholders benefit from the work because it has maintained or improved their homes; and
*   that the fact that the work has been done means that leaseholders will get a better price when they come to sell; and
*   that people that own their homes freehold have to find the money to meet costs of this kind.

To sum up the freeholder's position: the costs have been incurred; the work is for the benefit of the leaseholders; so the leaseholders must pay.

Leaseholders can point out in reply that someone that owns his home freehold can make his own choice when and how to do the repair; he can put up with a slightly leaking roof if he cannot afford to repair it. But freeholders of leasehold property have no such discretion: they are obliged under the lease to do their repairs promptly and if they did not would be liable to legal action by any leaseholder.

So it is difficult for leaseholders to object to the principle of service charges or to ask the freeholder to refrain from carrying out work or to delay it. In short, the purchase of a lease means the acceptance of a commitment to pay the appropriate share of costs.

But does this mean that leaseholders have no scope to challenge or query service charges? No; under sections 18 to 30 of the Landlord and Tenant Act 1985, they have extensive legal protection against improper or unreasonable charging by freeholders, and this is discussed later in the Chapter. First, however, we should look at how a typical service charge is made up.

The Components of a Service Charge
The lease will say how often service charges are levied: typically, six-monthly or annually. It is usual to collect the ground rent at the same time, but this is usually a fairly small component of the bill. The service charge proper will normally consist of three elements.

* **The management fee** is the charge made by the freeholder, or the freeholder's agent, to cover the administrative cost of providing the service and collecting the charge. Usually it will be much the same amount from one year to the next, but if major works have occurred the management fee will usually be higher to cover the extra costs of appointing and supervising contractors; 15% of the cost of the works is a common figure.

* **Direct costs (routine expenditure)** cover costs such as the supply of electricity to communal areas, building insurance, and the like. Again, these costs are likely to be fairly constant from year to year, so leaseholders know in advance roughly how much they are likely to have to pay.

* **Direct costs (exceptional expenditure)** cover costs that are likely to be irregular but heavy. They usually result from maintenance and repair, and it is because this component of

43

the service charge is so unpredictable that it gives rise to so many problems. Where a house has been divided into leasehold flats, the freeholder's costs will usually be similar to what a normal home owner would be obliged to pay; in other words, the costs may well be in the thousands (for a new roof, say) but are unlikely to be higher. Even so, a charge of £5000 for a new roof, albeit divided between three or four flats, is still a major cost from the point of view of the individual leaseholder, especially if it is unexpected. The situation can be far worse in blocks of flats, where the costs of essential repair and maintenance may run into millions. Replacement of worn-out lifts, for example, is notoriously costly; and costs arising from structural defects are likely to be higher still. Suppose it costs £2 million to remove asbestos from a block of forty flats: the average cost per flat is £50 000, a figure that may well exceed the value of the individual flats, and is likely to be beyond the reach of most leaseholders. The problem of exceptionally high service charges is looked at in greater detail at the end of the chapter.

Unreasonable Service Charges

a: General Principles

Sections 18 to 30 of the Landlord and Tenant Act 1985, as amended by subsequent legislation, grant substantial protection to leaseholders of residential property. This protection was introduced after complaints of exploitation by unscrupulous leaseholders, who were alleged to be carrying out unnecessary, or even fictitious, repairs at extravagant prices, whilst not providing the information that would have enabled leaseholders to query the bill. The general effect of the Act is to require freeholders to provide leaseholders with full information about service charges and to consult them before expensive works are carried out. It must be stressed, however, that although the Act protects leaseholders against sharp

44

practice by freeholders, and will prevent the recovery of **unreasonable** costs, it will support freeholders, provided they have

gone through the necessary formalities described below, in the recovery of their **reasonable** costs, even if those costs are high. To take the example used above of the removal of asbestos from a block of flats: the fact that the average cost per flat is as high as £50 000 does not, in itself, make the charge unreasonable - to make use of the Act, objecting leaseholders have to show, when they are notified that the work is to be carried out (not when the bills arrive), that it was not necessary or could have been carried out cheaper.

A few leases, namely those granted under the right to buy by local authorities or registered housing associations, have some additional protection under the Housing Act 1985 (see below), but sections 18 to 30 apply to all residential leases where the service charge depends on how much the freeholder spends. They set out the key rules that freeholders must observe in order to recover the cost, including overheads, of 'services, repairs or improvements, maintenance or insurance', as well as the freeholder's costs of management. Sections 18 to 30 only apply to service charges, not to other charges such as ground rent.

It should be noted that failure by leaseholders to pay the service charge does not relieve the freeholder of the obligation to provide the services. The freeholder's remedy is to sue the leaseholder for the outstanding charges, or even to seek forfeiture of the lease (see below).

Section 19 of the Act provides the key protection to leaseholders by laying down that service charges are recoverable only if they are 'reasonably incurred' and if the services or works are of a reasonable standard. This means that the charge:

45

- must relate to some form of service, repair, maintenance, improvement, or insurance that the freeholder is required to provide under the lease;
- must be reasonable (that is, the landlord may not recover costs incurred unnecessarily or extravagantly);
- may cover overheads and management costs only if these too are reasonable.

In addition, the charge must normally be passed on to the leaseholders within 18 months of being incurred, and in some cases the freeholder must consult leaseholders before spending the money. These points are covered below.

The Housing Act 1996 gave leaseholders new powers to refer service charges to the Leasehold Valuation Tribunal (LVT). This is covered below (*Challenging Service Charges*).

b: Consultation with Leaseholders
Section 20 provides extra protection where the cost of works is more than a certain limit. At the time of writing this is out for consultation, but the Government's current proposal is a cost of £250 or more to the leaseholder. Costs above this level are irrecoverable unless the freeholder has taken steps to inform and consult tenants, although there are a exceptions in special cases (see below). If the leaseholders are not represented by a recognised tenants' association (for which see below) these steps are as follows:

1 **Estimates** At least two estimates must be obtained, of which at least one must be from someone wholly unconnected from the freeholder (obviously a building firm that the freeholder owns or works for is not 'wholly unconnected'; nor is the freeholder's managing agent. Arguably, even a building firm with which the freeholder has no formal

46

connexion could be 'connected' with him if he gives it so much work that it depends on him and is thus subject to his influence)

2 **Notification to leaseholders** The freeholder must either display a copy of the estimates somewhere they are likely to be seen by everyone liable to pay the service charges or preferably send copies to everyone liable to pay the charge

3 **Consultation** The notification must describe the works to be carried out and must seek comments and observations, giving a deadline for replies and an address in the UK to which they may be sent. The deadline must be at least a month after the notice was sent or displayed.

4 **Freeholder's response** The freeholder must 'have regard' to any representations received. This does not mean, of course, that the freeholder must do what the leaseholders say. It does mean, however, that the freeholder must consider any comments received, and good freeholders often demonstrate that they have done so by sending a reasoned reply (i.e. not a form letter or bare acknowledgment, but a letter that responds specifically to any points made), even though the Act does not require them to.

It was mentioned above that there are special cases in which these requirements can be set aside. If a service charge is challenged, it is defence for the freeholder to show that the works were so urgent that there was no time for proper consultation. It is also possible for freeholders to enter into long term agreements to carry out works or provide services over a period of years; if so, they must consult before the agreement is entered into but they need not consult separately before each particular element of expenditure under the agreement. Finally, the LVT has a general power to set aside the usual consultation requirements if it seems fair to do so.

Section 20 is important because it gives the leaseholders notification of any unusual items in the offing and gives them an opportunity to raise any concerns and objections. If the leaseholder has any reservations at all, it is vital that they be put before the freeholder at this stage. It is unlikely, in the event of legal action later, that courts or LVTs will support a leaseholder that raised no objection until the bill arrived.

It is surprisingly common for freeholders and their agents to fail to comply with the requirements of section 20. This comment applies not only where the freehold is owned by an individual or a relatively small organisation (where mistakes might be more understandable) but also where the freeholder is a large, well resourced body like a local authority (which should be well able to understand and carry out its legal duties).

As a result leaseholders are often paying service charges that are not due, so all leaseholders should, before paying a service charge containing unusual items, ensure that section 20, if it applies, has been scrupulously followed. If not, they can refuse to pay.

c: Other Protection for Leaseholders
Grant-aided works: If the freeholder has received a grant towards the cost of carrying out the works, the amount must be deducted from the service charge levied on leaseholders.

Late charging: Service charge bills may not normally include costs incurred more than eighteen months earlier. The freeholder may, however, notify leaseholders within the eighteen month period that they will have to pay a certain cost, and then bill them later. This may happen if, for instance, the freeholder is in dispute with a contractor about the level of a bill or the standard of work.

Pre-charging: Sometimes a lease will contain a provision allowing the freeholder to make a charge to cover future costs besides those already incurred. This practice, which is perfectly lawful in itself, may be in the interests of the leaseholders by spreading over a longer period the cost of major works. It is, however, subject to the same overall requirement of reasonableness.

Court costs: Section 20C provides protection against a specific abuse of the service charge system by freeholders. Previously, freeholders tended to regard their legal costs as part of the process of managing the housing and thus as recoverable from leaseholders. Such an attitude is not necessarily unreasonable: if, for instance, the freeholder is suing a builder for poor work, he is, in effect, acting on behalf of all the leaseholders and it is fair that they should pay any legal costs. But suppose the freeholder were involved in legal proceedings against one of the leaseholders: if the leaseholder lost, he would probably to be ordered to pay the freeholder's costs as well as his own; but if the freeholder lost, and had to pay both his own and the leaseholder's costs, he could simply, under the previous law, recover the money as part of the management element in the service charge. This meant that the freeholder was able to pursue legal action against leaseholders without fear of heavy legal costs in the event of defeat, the very factor that deters most people from too ready a resort to law. To prevent this, section 20C allows leaseholders to seek an order that the freeholder's legal costs must not be counted towards service charges.

Service charges held on trust: Section 42 of the Landlord and Tenant Act 1987 further strengthened the position of leaseholders by laying down that the freeholder, or the freeholder's agent, must hold service charge monies in a suitable interest-bearing trust fund that will ensure that the money is protected and cannot be seized by the freeholder's creditors if the freeholder goes bankrupt or into liquidation. However, public sector freeholders, notably local authorities and registered housing associations, are exempt from this requirement.

Administration charges: These are the freeholder's costs incurred in complying with leaseholders' requests for information and approvals under the terms of the lease. All such charges must be reasonable. Any demand for administration charges must be accompanied by a summary of leaseholders' rights and obligations in relation to them. The LVT has the power to decide whether or not an administration charge is payable, and if so, to whom and by whom together with the amount, date payable and the manner in which it is paid.

Ground rent: Strictly, this is not part of the service charge but as it is usually collected along with it, it is covered here. It will be specified in the lease and is usually a fairly modest annual sum in the order of £50 or £100. Leaseholders should note that, unlike the service charge and most other charges, the ground rent is not intended to compensate the freeholder for any costs or trouble; it is simply a payment by which the leaseholder recognises that ultimately the property belongs to the freeholder. Therefore freeholders are under no obligation to demonstrate that it is reasonable. But it is not payable unless the landlord has issued a formal request for it, which must specify the amount of the payment, the date on which the leaseholder is liable to pay it and the date (if different) on which it would have been payable under the lease. The date for payment must be at least 30 days and not more than 60 days after the date of the notice.

Insurance: Usually, any insurance required under the lease will be Taken out by the freeholder and this is discussed below. Occasionally, however, the leaseholder will be required to take out insurance with a company nominated by the freeholder. If the leaseholder thinks he is getting a poor deal, he can apply to the county court or a Leasehold Valuation Tribunal which, if satisfied that the insurance is unsatisfactory or the premiums are unreasonably high, can order the freeholder to nominate another insurer.

'Period of Grace': When a dwelling is sold under the right to buy by a local authority or non-charitable housing association, the purchaser is given an estimate of service charges for the following five years. This estimate is the maximum recoverable during that time. Some purchasers under the right to buy have, however, had a very rude shock when the five year period of grace expires - see

Exceptionally High Service Charges below.
d: The role of a recognised tenants' association
The tenants who are liable to pay for the provision of services may, if they wish, form a recognised tenants' association (RTA) under section 29 of the Landlord and Tenant Act 1985. Note that leaseholders count as tenants for this purpose (see Chapter One, where it explained that legally the two terms are interchangeable). If the freeholder refuses to give a notice recognising the RTA, it may apply for recognition to any member of the local Rent Assessment Committee panel ('Rent Assessment Committee' is the official term for a Leasehold Valuation Tribunal when it is carrying out certain functions, not otherwise relevant to leaseholders, under the Rent Act 1977).

An important benefit of having a RTA is that it has the right, at the beginning of the consultation process, to recommend persons or organisations that should be invited to submit estimates. However, the freeholder is under no obligation to accept these recommendations.

Another advantage is that the RTA can, whether the freeholder likes it or not, appoint a qualified surveyor to advise on matters relating to service charges. The surveyor has extensive rights to inspect the freeholder's documentation and take copies, and can enforce these rights in court if necessary.

Against these benefits must be set the principal disadvantage of having a RTA, namely that it weakens the freeholder's obligation to consult individual leaseholders. Where there is a RTA, the freeholder, instead of having to supply copies of the estimates to all leaseholders (or place copies where they are likely to be seen), merely has to send them to the secretary of the RTA, and the individual leaseholders must make do with summaries.

Leaseholders - and for that matter, ordinary periodic tenants - should therefore weigh carefully the advantages and disadvantages of setting up a RTA. If they decide against, there is nothing to prevent them from forming an *unrecognised* tenants' (or leaseholders') association, which can represent their interests to the freeholder, provided that it is made clear that formal recognition under section 29 is not being sought.

Challenging Service Charges

The Landlord and Tenant Act not only allows leaseholders to take action against unreasonable behaviour by the freeholder; it also enables them to take the initiative. This is done in two ways: by giving leaseholders rights to demand information, and by allowing them to challenge the reasonableness of the charge.

Any demand for service charges must include details about leaseholders' rights and how they can challenge the charges. If this is not done the leaseholder may withhold payment without penalty.

a: Right to information

Freeholders must provide a written summary of costs counting towards the service charge. It must be sent to the leaseholder within six months of the end of the period it covers. The service charge need not be paid until the summary is provided.

The law lays down some minimum requirements for the summary. It must:

- cover all the costs incurred during the twelve months it covers, even if they were included in service charge bills of an earlier or later period (see above for late charging and pre-charging);
- show how the costs incurred by the freeholder are reflected in the service charges paid, or to be paid, by leaseholders;
- say whether it includes any work covered by a grant (see above);
- distinguish: (a) those costs incurred for which the freeholder was not billed during the period; (b) those for which he was billed and did not pay; (c) those for which he paid bills.

If it covers five or more dwellings, the summary must, in addition, be certified by a qualified accountant as being a fair summary, complying with the Act, and supported by appropriate documentation.

The purpose these rules is to put leaseholders in a position to challenge their service charges. After receiving the summary, the leaseholder has six months in which to ask the freeholder to make facilities available so that he can inspect the documents supporting the summary (bills, receipts, and so on) and take copies or extracts. The freeholder must make the facilities available within 21 days after such a request; the inspection itself must be free, although the freeholder can make a reasonable charge for the copies and extracts. Failure to provide these facilities, like failure to supply the summary, is punishable by a fine of up to £2500.

Very similar rules apply where the lease allows, or requires, the freeholder to take out insurance against certain contingencies, such as major repair, and to recover the premiums through the service charge. This is not unreasonable in itself and will, indeed, often be in the interests of leaseholders. The danger is, however, that the freeholder, knowing that the premiums are, in effect, being paid by someone else, has no incentive to shop around for the best deal. Section 30A of the Landlord and Tenant Act 1985 therefore lays down that leaseholders, or the secretary of the recognised tenants' association if there is one, may ask the freeholder for information about the policy. Failure to supply it, or to make facilities to inspect relevant documents available if requested to do so, is an offence incurring a fine of up to £2500.

It must be acknowledged that the rules allowing leaseholders to require information about service charges are, particularly in view of the £2500 fines, fairly onerous from the freeholder's point of view. It is the purpose of this book to inform leaseholders of their rights, not to make life difficult for freeholders: nevertheless, it must be admitted that if leaseholders wish to pursue a policy of confronting freeholders, and to cause them as much trouble as possible, sections 21, 22, and 30A offer plenty of scope.

b: Challenging a service charge
Any leaseholder liable to pay a service charge, and for that matter any freeholder levying one, may refer the charge to a Leasehold

Valuation Tribunal to determine its reasonableness. This may be done at any time, even when the service in question is merely a proposal by the freeholder (for instance, for future major works). But the LVT will not consider a service charge if:

- it has already been approved by a court; or
- if the leaseholder has agreed to refer it to arbitration; or
- if the leaseholder has agreed it.

The first of these exceptions is obvious and the second is unlikely to apply very often. The third one is the problem: leaseholders

should be careful, in their dealings with freeholders, to say or do nothing that could be taken to imply that they agree with any service charge that is in any way doubtful.

The LVT will consider:

- whether a service charge is payable and if so when, how, and by whom;
- whether the freeholder's costs of services, repairs, maintenance, insurance, or management are reasonably incurred;
- whether the services or works are of a reasonable standard; and
- whether any payment required in advance is reasonable.

The fees for application to a LVT can be obtained from the LVT and will usually change annually. Appeal against a LVT decision is not to the courts but to the Lands Tribunal.

By section 19 of the Landlord and Tenant Act 1985, any service charge deemed unreasonable by the LVT is irrecoverable by the freeholder. The determination of service charges by the LVT also plays an important part in the rules governing the use of forfeiture to recover service charges. It is to this that we now turn.

Forfeiture for Unpaid Service Charges

Forfeiture was mentioned at the end of Chapter Two. Briefly, it is the right of the freeholder to resume possession of the property if the leaseholder breaches the lease.

By section 81 of the Housing Act 1996, forfeiture for an unpaid service charge is available to the freeholder only if:
-    the leaseholder has agreed the charge; or
-    the charge has been upheld through post-dispute arbitration or by the Leasehold Valuation Tribunal or a court.

Regarding the first of these, it is necessary only to reiterate the warning to leaseholders to say or do nothing that could possibly be construed as representing their agreement to any service charge about whose legitimacy they have the slightest doubt.

Regarding the second, it should be noted that where the leaseholder has not agreed the service charge, proceedings before the LVT or a court or post-dispute arbitration are necessary before the freeholder can forfeit the lease.

A further requirement is that the amount of money involved must either exceed a certain amount or have been outstanding for a minimum period of time. The Government will set these limits by order. It is currently proposed that the minimum amount will be £350 and the minimum period three years, but this is yet to be confirmed. Note that it is necessary for only one of the requirements to be satisfied.

To sum up, before the leaseholder can forfeit:
- it must have been formally decided that the service charge is due,
- the amount must exceed the minimum amount or have been owed for the minimum time, and
- a section 146 notice must have been served (but this requirement does not apply if the service charge is reserved as rent).

The freeholder can still begin the process by issuing a section 146 notice (see Chapter Two) but it must state that the forfeiture cannot proceed until the requirements of section 81 have been met.

It remains to be seen how these new provisions will operate in practice. Their purpose is to prevent freeholders from using the draconian threat of forfeiture to pressurise leaseholders into paying disputed service charges, and to this extent the position of leaseholders has been greatly strengthened. The danger is that freeholders may respond by getting disputed charges before the LVT as quickly as possible so that forfeiture becomes available if the charges are upheld. Another concern is that some leaseholders, faced with service charges they are unwilling to pay but about which there is no dispute, may be unable to resist the temptation to invent spurious grounds for objection in order to deprive the freeholder of the weapon of forfeiture; this tactic is likely to provoke even relatively easy-going freeholders into legal action.

Once the leaseholder has agreed the service charge or it has been upheld by the LVT or a court or through arbitration, forfeiture becomes a serious threat and in this situation the advice can only be to pay the charge if at all possible. If, however, the leaseholder is unable to pay he may find it helpful to contact his mortgagee (if any). For the mortgagee, forfeiture is a disaster because it is likely to be left with a large unsecured debt on its hands, so many mortgagees in this situation will pay the service charges and add the cost to the outstanding mortgage. This does not solve the leaseholder's long term problem - that his lease commits him to payments he is unable to meet - but it will give him a little breathing space and may enable him to sell up and pay off his debts.

Some leaseholders, especially those of longer standing, may be living on fixed incomes and have very little cash to spare, even though their property is quite valuable. Sometimes their mortgage has been paid off altogether; even if it is still outstanding, it will probably be very small in relation to the value of the property. Leaseholders that find themselves in this 'property-rich, cash-poor' situation may find it helpful to look at equity release schemes, operated by a number of financial institutions.

Exceptionally High Service Charges
So far this Chapter has focused on service charges of normal proportions that, however unforeseen and unwelcome they may be, should be within the means of the great majority of leaseholders. A minority of leaseholders, however, face the much more serious problem of consistently very high service charges. Where the cause is sharp practice by the freeholder, or failure to observe the legal requirements, the leaseholder can look for protection to the Landlord and Tenant Act as described above. Often, however, the freeholder is not to blame: rather, the problem is that the work is genuinely necessary and unavoidably expensive. In this situation, and provided the landlord carefully follows the procedures laid down, the Landlord and Tenant Act offers no protection.

In what sort of housing is this most likely to occur? It is more likely to affect flats than houses because flats tend to contain potentially very expensive components such as lifts or communal arrangements for heating or ventilation. They are also more likely to have been built using construction methods or designs in vogue at one time but since found to lead to serious maintenance problems and high costs, whereas house building seems to be innately conservative and resistant to innovation: for instance, many blocks of flats contain asbestos, but very few houses.

All these problems apply to flats in general, but there is an additional problem with blocks of flats owned by local authorities and housing associations: namely that, unlike blocks of flats developed by commercial owners for sale, they are likely to combine rented properties, let to periodic tenants in the usual way, with leasehold properties, sold at some point in the past under the right to buy or some similar scheme. These 'mixed managed' blocks present special problems for both categories of resident as well as the freeholder.

The problems can be shown by taking a hypothetical example. **MUNICIPAL HEIGHTS** is a 15-storey tower block developed by the London Borough of Walford in the 1960s (when such things were fashionable). It contains 75 flats of which 60 are rented and 15 have been bought under the right to buy. In recent years its condition has deteriorated markedly: the lifts, having long exceeded their projected 25-year working life, have become hopelessly unreliable and urgently need to be replaced; the stairways, landings, and other communal areas need complete refurbishment; the windows need to be replaced; and asbestos has been found in the block. The tenants are understandably up in arms about their living conditions and are demanding action by the Council. The leaseholders, on the other hand, although also concerned about the state of the block, are well aware that the cost of necessary works has been reliably estimated at £3 000 000, working out to an average of £40 000 per dwelling, a sum none of them can possibly afford, and more than the value of the flats. The Council sympathises with their predicament but, on the other hand, some of the tenants are threatening it with legal action for failure to carry out its repairing obligations, and others are getting up a campaign to vote out the sitting Councillors in the forthcoming elections. So the Council, having carried out the consultation exercise required by the Landlord and Tenant Act, decides to go ahead and carry out the repairs. Now the Council's problem is that if it seeks to recover £40 000 each from the leaseholders, they will be unable to pay and the Council will have little option but to take legal action against them up to and including forfeiture; whereas if it makes no such attempt the debt will have to be met from elsewhere in the Housing Revenue Account, which, since Councils are no longer allowed to top up the HRA from general funds, means that it will be paid by the rents of Council tenants throughout the Borough, to which the Walford Federation of Tenants' Associations strongly objects.

One way out is for the government to come to the rescue. Sometimes, a council can obtain grants meeting some or all of the cost of improving run-down property. If this happened at Municipal Heights, the leaseholders' contributions could be considerably reduced, or even eliminated entirely. But funds of this kind are not available automatically; they have to be applied for, and come from a cash-limited budget. If the Council cannot get government funding, what then?

Clearly, there is no satisfactory way to resolve this problem. In a privately developed block, occupied wholly by leaseholders, the freeholder might possibly be prevailed upon to delay the repairs for a time if the leaseholders are prepared to put up with the poor conditions; but the Council can hardly be expected to take the same view when most of the residents are periodic tenants. Both the Council and the periodic tenants are likely to argue that the leaseholders are being asked to do no more than they agreed to do when they bought their leases. So the problems affecting Municipal Heights, and similar developments all over the country, are likely to rumble on for many years.

It is possible that the leaseholders will have redress if they can persuade a court that the local authority acted in bad faith at the time of the sale; if, for instance, Walford Council was well aware, but did not disclose, that there were, or might be, serious structural problems with Municipal Heights.

In most cases, however, Councils will be able to say, quite truthfully, that they had no idea of the problem when the sale took place, in which case the court is likely to apply the established legal principle of *caveat emptor* - 'let the buyer beware'.

All this book can do is warn prospective leaseholders of the serious problems that can arise in a minority of cases, and suggest some of the questions that they should ask before signing the lease.

1   **What is the condition of the building as a whole?** No one would buy a house, or an individual flat, without looking closely at its condition and estimating how much money it may need to have spent on it. But, when a flat is being bought, whether it is purpose-built or a conversion, it is equally important to look at the entire building of which it forms a part. The vendor should be asked for copies of past service charges, the freeholder should be asked whether major work is likely in the foreseeable future and what it is likely to cost, and an independent surveyor should be asked to report.

2   **What is the leaseholder's liability?** The lease will specify what the leaseholder must pay for. Sometimes it will require

him to contribute to things from which he does not benefit. For example, it is common for even ground floor leaseholders to be expected to contribute to the costs of the lifts; and some leaseholders, having paid out of their own pockets to replace their windows, are outraged to discover, when the freeholder has the windows of the whole block renewed, that they are required to pay a share of the cost. Provisions such as these are much resented by many leaseholders, who argue that they are unfair; but the time to object to such unfairness is before signing the lease, not many years later when the bills come in. It is therefore essential that anyone proposing to enter into a lease should first consult a solicitor.

3   **Is there a 'period of grace' or other safeguard?** Right to buy leases contain an estimate of service charges for five years following the sale and that is the maximum that the Council may charge. Many purchasers, reassured by this, have signed the lease without paying much attention to the likely level of service charges thereafter, expecting perhaps to have sold at a profit and moved on before the five years expire. If so, they have been reminded of what many people forgot during the 1980s: that property prices can go down as well as up. In short, it is unwise to rely on a 'period of grace' to provide anything other than short-term relief; and in particular it is unwise to speculate on the future behaviour of the housing market.

4   **What are the prospects for resale?** Traditionally, the homeowner's last resort in the face of overwhelming financial problems is to sell up in the expectation that the proceeds will suffice to pay off the mortgage, settle other outstanding debts such as service charges, and still leave something over. The stagnant property market of the early 1990s upset many

calculations of this kind, but the much stronger market of recent years means that mortgages are often appreciably less than the value of the property, so for many people selling up offers a way out. So it is important to assess the salability of the dwelling by asking whether future purchasers are likely to be put off by anything about the flat itself or the block and district to which it belongs, and above all whether mortgage lenders are likely to look on it favourably.

-4-

ENFRANCHISEMENT AND EXTENSION OF LEASES

What Are Enfranchisement and Extension?

Chapter One set out the legal theory underlying the relationship between freeholder and leaseholder, and explained that a lease must be limited in time and that, in principle, at the end of that time the lease finishes and the property reverts to the freeholder.

It has always been, and still is, open to the freeholder and the leaseholder to negotiate some different arrangement. For instance, they might agree that the freeholder will buy the unexpired term of the lease from the leaseholder: but, because the freeholder and the leaseholder cannot be the same person, this will have the effect of extinguishing the lease and the leave the freeholder on sole possession of the land as if the lease had never existed. Alternatively, the freeholder might agree to sell the freehold to the leaseholder: again, and for the same reason, this will extinguish the lease, but this time it is the former leaseholder that will be left in sole freehold possession. The sale of the freehold to the leaseholder is called 'enfranchisement' of the lease, because it is freed, or 'enfranchised', from the overriding freehold, and replaces it. A further possibility is that the freeholder and leaseholder may agree to extend the lease beyond its original term. If agreements of this kind are negotiated, it is entirely for the freeholder and leaseholder to settle the conditions and the price.

In recent years, however, the law has forced freeholders, in certain circumstances, to sell freeholds or extend leases, whether they wish to or not. This has been done by three pieces of legislation: the

Leasehold Reform Act 1967, the Landlord and Tenant Act 1987, and the Leasehold Reform, Housing and Urban Development Act 1993 (although all three Acts have been amended by later legislation, particularly the Housing Act 1996 and the Commonhold and Leasehold Reform Act 2002). The Acts are dealt with in the order they were passed, which means that the most important right - that of leaseholders of flats - is left to last. This is fitting, because, as is explained below, it was a Parliamentary afterthought; the Government originally had no intention of granting such an important right.

But before looking at the legislation, it is important to establish why extension and enfranchisement are important to the average leaseholder.

Extension of a Lease Some enlightened freeholders automatically extend the lease whenever it is assigned, so that if a lease that was originally granted for 125 years is assigned after 30, the assignee gets a lease not for 95 years, as one might expect, but for 125. From the leaseholder's point of view, such an arrangement is extremely valuable because otherwise the lease represents a wasting asset, whose value will drop sharply as the end of the term approaches. The arrangement can also benefit the freeholder by making the lease more valuable at the time of its original sale. But most leases are unaffected by assignment and would expire on the originally determined date were it not for legislation that obliges freeholders, in certain circumstances, to grant a fresh 90 year lease to the leaseholder: this is described below.

Individual Enfranchisement of a Lease Legislation, described below, now allows the leaseholder to acquire the freehold, in certain circumstances, whether or not the freeholder agrees. If not for this, the leaseholder would find that his home had reverted to the

66

ownership of the freeholder at the end the lease and he would have to buy it back (assuming the freeholder were willing to sell). The freeholder is, however, entitled to compensation.

Collective Enfranchisement of Leases   The problem with leasehold enfranchisement is that the property concerned must be capable of being held on a freehold basis. Where it stands on a distinct and definable piece of land this does not present a problem: the freehold of the land is transferred to the leaseholder and, as explained in Chapter One, any buildings on it are automatically transferred too. But if the property is only part of a larger building, it may not be attached to its own unique piece of land in the same way, so individual enfranchisement is not available to flat owners. If they wish to enfranchise, therefore, they have to agree among themselves that a single person or body will buy the freehold on behalf of all of them, while they continue to hold leases of their individual flats.

This is called 'collective enfranchisement', although this term is misleading because technically the leases have not been enfranchised at all: all that has happened is a change from the original freeholder to a new one nominated by the leaseholders. Since the passage of the Commonhold and Leasehold Reform Act 2002, this new freeholder has to be a special type of organisation called a 'Right to Enfranchise' (or 'RtE') company.

Rights to Enfranchise and Extend Leases: General Principles
The remainder of this Chapter sets out what rights leaseholders have if they wish to extend or enfranchise their leases. It is stressed at the outset, however, that anyone contemplating such a step should obtain independent legal advice from a solicitor, and in most cases also from a valuer. This applies not only if the lease is being enfranchised or extended under one of the Acts, but also if it is

67

being done voluntarily by agreement with the freeholder. The issues involved are potentially very complex and attempting to deal with them without expert advice could put your home at risk.

The Acts are available to what they describe as 'qualifying tenants': but the exact meaning of the term varies depending which right is being exercised under which Act. Usually, but not always, the term is defined in a way that excludes ordinary tenants and confines it to leaseholders. The key issue is the existence of a long lease (see below). Other former tests, relating to residence or the amount of rent, were abolished by the 2002 Act.

A Long Lease For most purposes under the Acts, the leaseholder must own a lease originally granted for at least 21 years. Note that this is the term when the lease was granted, not the period it still has to run, so that a 99 year lease granted in 1910 is still a long lease in 2003 even though it has only six years to go. Recent legislation has put an end to a number of devices formerly inserted into leases by freeholders in order to avoid having to extend or enfranchise leases.

Some were bizarre: leases were made terminable on extraneous events, such as royal marriages or deaths, because the lease was not regarded as long if it depended on an event that could occur at any time. These evasions have been of no effect since the 1993 Act, which provides that leases containing them shall be treated as long leases.

Exemptions There are various exemptions from the Acts.
- If the freeholder is a charitable housing trust and the dwelling is provided as part of its charitable work, the leaseholder can neither extend nor enfranchise the lease (unless the charity agrees).
- The Acts do not apply to business leases. This applies even if

a dwelling is included: for instance, if the lease of a shop includes the flat above it.

- The Acts do not apply if the property is within the precincts of a cathedral or owned by the Crown (however, it is possible that the Crown authorities will agree to a voluntary extension or enfranchisement of the lease). Some properties owned by the National Trust are also exempt.

- Other exemptions apply not across the board but to particular types of transaction. These are covered as the various Acts are discussed below.

Leasehold Reform Act 1967: Leases of Houses

The first legislation to deal with leasehold extension and enfranchisement was the Leasehold Reform Act 1967. This Act is still in force, but is not relevant to most residential leaseholders, who will get more benefit from later legislation. It can therefore be dealt with fairly briefly.

The Act relates only to residential leases of houses - not flats. With certain exceptions, a leaseholder qualifies to use it if he has held for at least two years a lease originally granted for 21 years or more. The Act allows qualifying leaseholders to acquire the freehold of their homes, or, if they prefer, extend the lease for 50 years.

The usual exemptions (see above) apply to the 1967 Act. In addition, it does not apply to most shared ownership leases granted by housing associations.

Most leaseholders qualifying to make use of the 1967 Act have long since done so, because the benefits of owning the freehold outweigh the drawback of having to pay the freeholder the difference (usually not very great) between the freehold and leasehold value of the house.

Generally speaking, therefore, remaining leasehold houses will be those to which the Act does not apply, either because the freeholder is exempt or because the house is attached to other property. The last point is an important limitation on the 1967 Act: if the land on which the house stands is shared by any other property not covered by the lease, however small it may be compared with the house, the Act cannot be used. It may, however, be possible for the leaseholder of such a house to use the new rights in the Leasehold Reform, Housing and Urban Development Act 1993.

The procedure for enfranchisement under the 1967 Act is as follows.

- The leaseholder serves a notice on the freeholder stating that he wishes to claim the freehold (or extend the lease). This notice should give particulars of the property and the lease.

- Within two months, the freeholder must send a counter notice that either accepts the leaseholder's claim or gives reasons for rejecting it. The freeholder may ask the leaseholder for a deposit of £25 or thrice the annual ground rent, whichever is more, and for proof that he holds the lease and meets the residence test. The leaseholder has 14 days to produce the money and 21 days to produce the proof.

- If the freeholder does not submit a counter notice within two months, the leaseholder's claim is automatically accepted. If the freeholder's counter notice unfairly rejects the leaseholder's claim, the leaseholder may apply to the county court.

Obviously, the freeholder is justified in rejecting the claim if the property does not come under the Act or if the leaseholder does not qualify. In addition, the freeholder may reject the claim if he acquired the house before 18th February 1966 and needs the house, on expiry of the lease, as a home for himself or a member of his family. He may also refuse to extend the lease (but not to enfranchise it) if he plans to redevelop the property.

Once it has been established that the leaseholder may enfranchise, a price must be agreed; if this is not possible, it will be set by a leasehold valuation tribunal. The Act lays down that the price should be the value of the freehold if it were being sold willingly but on the assumption that the lease were continuing and would be renewable under the Act. In effect, this formula means that the leaseholder is obliged to pay for what he is acquiring (the freehold) but not for what he has already got (the lease). Once a price has been agreed, or set by tribunal, either the freeholder or the leaseholder has one month to serve a notice on the other requiring him to complete. The freeholder must convey the freehold as a fee simple absolute, or (as a non-lawyer would say) outright.

Landlord and Tenant Act 1987: First Refusal and Mismanagement

The Landlord and Tenant Act 1987 was chiefly concerned with enabling leaseholders to protect themselves against unreasonable service charges, and it made numerous amendments to tighten the rules originally laid down in the Landlord and Tenant Act 1985 (see Chapter Three).

In addition, it granted leaseholders the important right of first refusal if the freehold of their property is sold. It also allowed leaseholders to acquire the freehold if the property is being mismanaged: however, this right is little used because of the difficult procedures involved, and although it remains on the statute book it is likely to fall into complete disuse because the 1993 Act has now given leaseholders the same right without having to prove mismanagement.

a: First refusal

The right of first refusal was granted in order to stop the practice of selling freeholds, without any reference to the leaseholders or other occupiers, from one person or organisation to another so that leaseholders were often completely in the dark about who the ultimate freeholder was (when this sort of thing went on the eventual freeholder often turned out to be a company existing on paper only and based somewhere completely inaccessible like the Cayman Islands - see Chapter Two for legislation passed at the same time forcing freeholders to give their name and an address in the UK for the service of legal notices). The right of first refusal remains important because it is sometimes available when ordinary collective enfranchisement, under the 1993 Act, is not possible.

The 1987 Act says that if the freeholder intends to sell the freehold he must first offer it to the leaseholders and other qualifying tenants. There are, however, some exceptions: the Act does not apply if the freeholder is selling to a member of his family, or if he lives in the block himself; nor does it apply if the block is not chiefly residential. In addition, virtually all public sector freeholders are excluded from the Act: this means local authorities, registered housing associations, and various other bodies. It is, however, unlikely that this sort of body will wish to sell its freehold. But if none of these exceptions applies, and if the majority of qualifying tenants (including leaseholders) wish to buy, they must be given the opportunity to meet the freeholder's price. For the purpose of defining a 'majority' there can be only one qualifying tenant in respect of each flat: in other words, joint tenants (or joint leaseholders) have only one 'vote' between them, and must agree between themselves how it will be used.

'Qualifying tenants' are:
• tenants entitled to a Fair Rent under the 1977 Rent Act: that is,

most tenants of self-contained dwellings holding a tenancy originally granted on or before 14th January 1989, but excluding council tenants; and

• leaseholders, except for business leaseholders (the normal 21 year minimum does not apply).

If the qualifying tenants and freeholder cannot agree terms for the sale, the freeholder is able to sell to someone else. However, the qualifying tenants must be informed of this sale and, most importantly, of the price. They then have the right to buy the freehold from the new owner at whatever price he paid. This is designed to stop the original freeholder from asking the qualifying tenants for an excessive price that they are bound to reject, then selling to someone else at a lower price. Similarly, if the freeholder carries out a sale without informing the qualifying tenants, they have the right to buy from the new freeholder for the same price that he paid. Procedure under the 1987 for the right of first refusal is as follows.

*   The freeholder notifies all qualifying tenants of his desire to sell and of the price at which he is willing to do so (including any non-monetary element). The notice must state the proposed method of sale: for instance, by conveyance or by auction.

*   The freeholder must give the qualifying tenants at least two months to respond; and, if they say they wish to buy, at least a further two months (28 days if the sale is to be by auction) to come up with a nominee purchaser to acquire the freehold on their behalf. This could conceivably be in an individual or an organisation that already exists, but is much likelier to be a company set up specially for the purpose by the qualifying tenants, and under their control.

*   During this period, the landlord and the qualifying tenants may wish to take the opportunity to negotiate the price.

*   If a majority of the qualifying tenants have put forward a nominee purchaser and agreed with the freeholder on a price, the freeholder may not sell to anyone else.

*   If the qualifying tenants fail to put forward a nominee purchaser, or if a mutually acceptable price is not agreed, the freeholder has twelve months to sell to someone else in accordance with the original notice (by auction, if that was the method specified; and in any other case for a price not less than that originally offered to the qualifying tenants). If no sale has taken place within twelve months, the freeholder must start the procedure again from scratch if he wishes to sell.

b: Mismanagement: the right to enfranchise

As mentioned above, the 1987 Act is designed mainly to protect leaseholders against mismanagement and sharp practice by freeholders. It therefore gives them the power of collective enfranchisement against a freeholder guilty of serious or repeated breach of his obligations. The power is available to long leaseholders, but a leaseholder does not qualify to use this part of the Act if he owns long leases of three or more flats in the block.

Moreover, this part of the 1987 Act does not apply where the freeholder is the Crown or a public body such as a local authority or a registered housing association. Nor does it apply when the freeholder resides in the property himself. It is available only where two-thirds or more of the flats in the block are let on long leases, and in blocks of ten flats or fewer a higher proportion is required. The court can make an order transferring the freehold to the leaseholders' nominee only if a manager appointed (see Chapter

Two) by a court or LVT has controlled the premises for at least two years, unless the leaseholders can show both

- that the freeholder is and is likely to remain in breach of his obligations under the lease; and
- that the mere appointment of a manager would be an inadequate remedy.

All these restrictions suggest that the Act envisages that enfranchisement on grounds of mismanagement is very much a last resort; indeed, it is necessary for the leaseholders to take their case to court and get permission before they can proceed. The right was seldom used and, although it remains available in theory, in practice it has been superseded by the 1993 Act, which gives most leaseholders the right of collective enfranchisement whatever the standard of management and with no need for a court order. Nevertheless, it is just possible there is a body of leaseholders somewhere willing to use the 1987 Act rather than the 1993 Act. The procedures for collective enfranchisement following mismanagement are therefore briefly set out here, with a warning that the general recommendation to employ a solicitor applies with special emphasis if this route is chosen.

- At least two-thirds of the qualifying leaseholders must serve a preliminary notice informing the freeholder that they intend to go to court to acquire the freehold. The notice must give the names and addresses of the leaseholder and the grounds for their application; the freeholder should also be given a reasonable deadline to rectify the problems if it is possible for him to do so.

- The leaseholders must apply to the court, giving their reasons for dissatisfaction and requesting an order to transfer the freehold to their nominee purchaser (probably, as with other forms of collective enfranchisement, a company set up for the purpose).

- If satisfied that it is fair to do so, the court will transfer the block to the nominee purchaser. The price will have to be agreed by the leaseholders and the freeholder; or, if (as is likely) this is not possible, by a Leasehold Valuation Tribunal. The price will be the value of the freehold on the assumption that all the leases are to continue: there will be no additional 'marriage value' (see below), and this is one of the few reasons for preferring to use the 1987 Act rather than the 1993 Act.

Leasehold Reform, Housing and Urban Development Act 1993: Collective Enfranchisement and Lease Extension

The 1993 Act greatly extended the rights of leaseholders: its passage through Parliament was, indeed, strongly contested by large private freeholders, who claimed that it was unfair to them as property owners. It made a number of adjustments, dealt with above, to existing rights under the 1967 and 1987 Acts; in addition, it created two new rights for leaseholders of flats. These are the right to collective enfranchisement, and the right to extend individual leases.

a: Collective enfranchisement under the 1993 Act

In outline, the right to collective enfranchisement under the 1993 Act is similar to, but much easier than, collective enfranchisement under the 1987 Act. Under both schemes, qualifying leaseholders choose a purchaser to whom the freeholder can be forced to sell; but under the 1993 Act there is no need for a court order and no need to show that there has been mismanagement.

The 1993 Act is available to long leaseholders, provided that at least two-thirds of the flats are let on long leases and at least half the eligible leaseholders are involved.

However, the block may not be enfranchised if it falls within the normal exemptions, or if it is not chiefly residential, or if it is a house converted into four flats or fewer with a resident freeholder who owned the freehold before the conversion. Even if there is a resident freeholder, however, the scheme applies to houses converted into five flats or more and to purpose-built blocks even if they contain only two flats.

There are special provisions for any parts of the building that are occupied by people or organisations other than qualifying leaseholders. Some flats may be let to periodic tenants, for instance, and a block that faces a main road may well contain shop units on the ground floor. Any such parts may, and in some cases must, be leased back to the original freeholder when the block is acquired. 'Leaseback', as it is called, is mandatory for any flats let to periodic tenants (secure or assured) by a local authority or a registered housing association. This means that they can continue as council (or association) tenants, and do not lose any legal rights. It is up to the freeholder (not the leaseholders) whether he wants a leaseback of other flats or premises, such as business units or flats occupied by non-qualifying leaseholders. Unless the parties agree otherwise, leaseback is for 999 years at a notional rent - in other words, on terms typical of residential leases, and discussed in Chapters One and Two.

The leaseholders must choose a purchaser. Formerly, this could be any individual or organisation that had the confidence of the others and was willing to undertake the role. The 2002 Act has, however, tightened the rules by providing that only a 'Right to Enfranchise' ('RtE') company can take over the freehold. This protects leaseholders' rights by ensuring that the enfranchisee is a body in which they all have a right to be involved, but the Government has taken powers to lay down what the constitution of the RtE company must be, and it is likely that many leaseholders will find the prescribed constitution unwieldy and inflexible.

Setting up and running the RtE company is only one of the responsibilities in which collective enfranchisement will involve leaseholders. They will also have to pay both their own and the freeholder's legal and professional costs. And above all, they must pay the purchase price of the freehold, which, unless they come to an agreement with the freeholder, will be decided by a leasehold valuation tribunal in accordance with rules laid down in the Act. These say that the price consists of two components: the open market value and the 'marriage value'.

According to the formula in the Act, the **open market value** should reflect the income the freeholder would have received from rents plus the prospect of regaining possession of the parts of the building currently let. How much this is will depend on how the building is being used now. If, as will often be the case, it consists wholly of flats let on long leases with many years to run, the open market value will probably be low because ground rents are usually very modest and the prospect of regaining possession is a distant one and of correspondingly little value. But if the building contains lucrative business or periodic tenancies, perhaps quite short term, and if the freeholder elects not to have these leased back, the open market value will be substantial.

The other component in the price, the **'marriage value'**, is based on the assumption that, combined (as they will be after enfranchisement), the leases and the freehold have a greater value than they would if sold separately. The Act says the freeholder is entitled to half this amount. In most cases, however, especially where the leases have a long time to run, the marriage value will be low, and where a lease has more than 80 years to run the marriage value will be disregarded. Altogether the costs of enfranchisement may be considerable. It is therefore prudent for leaseholders to explore the ground before committing themselves. This can be done by any qualifying leaseholder by serving a notice on the freeholder (or whomever the leaseholder pays rent to) under section 11 of the Act. Such a notice obliges the freeholder to disclose, within 28 days, information that will be relevant to any sale, such as title deeds, surveyor's reports, planning restrictions, and so on. This will allow the leaseholders to take an informed view of whether they wish to go for collective enfranchisement and, if so, on what terms. At this stage, they should take their time and think it over carefully, for if they proceed further they will be obliged to pay the freeholder's legal costs if they later decide to withdraw.

It may be appropriate, too, at this stage, for the leaseholders to ask the freeholder whether he is prepared to consider a voluntary sale without forcing all concerned to go through the somewhat elaborate procedures laid down by the 1993 Act. A reasonable freeholder, since he will be aware that he can be forced to sell anyway, may well be willing to discuss this.

If the leaseholders decide to go ahead with collective enfranchisement under the 1993 Act, they must form a 'Right to Enfranchise' ('RtE') company. The purpose of the company is to act as the vehicle for the enfranchisement and subsequently to own the freehold of the block.

Every RtE company has to operate in accordance with a constitution (the 'memorandum and articles') laid down by Government. The aim is to ensure that all leaseholders have a fair chance to take part, but it is likely that many leaseholders will find that the constitution laid down for them is extremely bureaucratic and unwieldy, especially when it is remembered that many enfranchisements will be carried out in small blocks where they may be only a dozen leaseholders or even fewer.

All qualifying leaseholders are entitled to be members of the RtE company, but in practice it is controlled by 'participating members', namely those leaseholders that have served on the company a 'participation notice'. When the company is set up all qualifying leaseholders must be sent a formal notice inviting them to participate by serving such a notice. Once the enfranchisement takes place, membership of the RtE company is confined to participating members.

The RtE company serves an initial notice (also called a 'section 13 notice') giving the names and addresses of the leaseholders involved and exactly specifying what property they wish to enfranchise and which parts, if any, they will lease back. The notice must also propose a price, and give the freeholder at least two months to reply. Once the initial notice has been served, the freeholder may not sell the freehold to any third party.

From now on, the RtE company handles proceedings on behalf of the leaseholders. The freeholder may require the RtE company to provide evidence to show that the participating leaseholders are qualified under the Act. If the RtE company does not respond within 21 days, the freeholder may in some circumstances treat the initial notice as being withdrawn.

By the date specified in the initial notice, the freeholder must serve a counter notice either accepting the leaseholders' right to enfranchise or giving reasons for rejecting it. The freeholder must also state whether he accepts the details of the leaseholders' proposal as regards price and exactly what is to be included in the sale, and must say whether he wishes to lease back any parts of the property (in addition to those where leaseback is mandatory). The freeholder may refuse to exercise his right to lease back parts of the premises let on lucrative business lets because the effect of this will be to increase the price and, perhaps, deter the leaseholders from continuing. In the unlikely event that most of the leaseholders' leases have less than five years to run, the freeholder has the right to stop the enfranchisement if he can satisfy a court that he intends to redevelop the block.

The intention of the Act is that after the freeholder's counter notice the parties will attempt to resolve any differences, so that the sale of the freehold can proceed on agreed terms. Often, however, agreement will be impossible and in that case the matters in dispute are referred to a leasehold valuation tribunal. Such a referral must take place at least two months, and not more than six months, after the freeholder's counter notice; if no agreement is reached, and no referral made, after six months, the initial notice will be deemed withdrawn.

Once the terms have been settled, the parties have two months to exchange contracts. At the end of this time, the nominee purchaser has a further two months to ask a court to transfer the freehold on the terms agreed (or determined by the tribunal); or the freeholder may ask the court to rule that the initial notice shall be treated as being withdrawn.

To sum up, the procedure is complex and demanding, which is why it has been little used even though several years have passed since it became available under the 1993 Act. The 2002 Act has made the process more favourable to leaseholders in some ways, but these improvements are more than offset by the further layer of difficulty added by the new requirement to set up a RtE company. All in all, it seems likely that these procedures will not be much used, but their existence may be helpful in persuading freeholders to negotiate seriously if leaseholders want to buy the freehold.

b: Lease extension under the 1993 Act

Although the right to collective enfranchisement, as created by the 1993 Act, is of great importance because it makes a fundamental shift in the relationship between freeholders and leaseholders, the complex procedures mean that it is likely to be relatively seldom used. On the other hand, the right to a new lease, which was also created (for flat owners) by the 1993 Act, is likely to prove of immense practical benefit to thousands of leaseholders, not least because it can be exercised on an individual basis. It is ironic that this, the most valuable right leaseholders derive from the 1993 Act, was something of a Parliamentary afterthought. The original intention was to create the right to collective enfranchisement, with individual lease extensions as very much a second best option available only to leaseholders that for some reason were disqualified from collective enfranchisement. But as the legislation made its way through Parliament the right to extend leases was granted to more and more categories of leaseholder, and by the time the Act became law it had become a general right.

The principle is similar to the right to lease extension that house owners enjoy under the 1967 Act. Anyone that has owned for at least two years a long lease of a flat qualifies to extend it under the 1993 Act. The former low rent test and residence test were abolished by the 2002 Act. The freeholder is required to grant a new lease running for the remainder of the term of the old lease plus an additional 90 years, so that if the old lease had 40 years to go the new one will be granted for 130. In other respects, however, the terms of the new lease will be the same as, or very similar to, the old one.

The leaseholder will have to pay the freeholder a sum consisting of two components calculated in accordance with rules set out in the Act. The first represents the reduction in the market value of the freehold that results because the freeholder will now have to wait to regain possession for 90 years longer than would otherwise have been the case. The less time the old lease had to run, the higher this component is likely to be. The second component is the 'marriage value', reflecting the higher value of a longer lease. As with collective enfranchisement, the freeholder is entitled to 50% of the marriage value, but it is disregarded altogether if the old lease has more than 80 years to go.

A leaseholder who is contemplating a lease extension should begin by serving a preliminary notice on the freeholder. This has the same function as with collective enfranchisement: it commits the leaseholder to nothing, but requires the freeholder to supply within 28 days the information that will enable the leaseholder to decide whether to go ahead.

The procedure is modelled on that for collective enfranchisement:

- The leaseholder serves an initial notice (a 'section 42 notice') on the freeholder. This must give details of the property concerned as well as of the leaseholder and his claim to qualify to use the 1993 Act. It must state how much the leaseholder proposes to pay, and set a date, at least two months ahead, by which the freeholder must reply. Once the notice has been served, the leaseholder must allow the freeholder to have access to the flat for the purpose of valuation.

- The freeholder must either agree that the leaseholder qualifies under the Act, or give reasons for disagreeing. If the freeholder agrees that the leaseholder is qualified to extend the lease, he may still suggest a that price of the new lease, or its other terms, should be different to the leaseholder's proposals. The freeholder can go to court for permission to reject the extension entirely if the current lease has less than five years to run and the freeholder then intends to redevelop the property.

- The freeholder and leaseholder should then attempt to resolve any differences by negotiation. If agreement is not reached, the question may be referred to the leasehold valuation tribunal at lease two months, and not less than six months, after the freeholder's counter notice. If, six months after the counter notice, there is neither an agreement nor a referral to a tribunal, the leaseholder's initial notice will be deemed withdrawn. In this event the leaseholder is liable for any reasonable expenses incurred by the freeholder.

- Once the terms are settled, either by negotiation or by the tribunal, the parties have two months to exchange contracts. If exchange does not take place during this period, the leaseholder has a further two months to apply to court for an order extending the lease on the terms agreed (or laid down by a tribunal).

It should be noted that collective enfranchisement takes priority over individual lease extensions, so that the effect of an initial notice of collective enfranchisement is to freeze, for the time being, any current claims to extend leases. If the collective enfranchisement fails to go ahead, the extension claims resume where they left off.

-5-

COMMONHOLDS AND FLYING FREEHOLDS

In conclusion, it may be useful to look at how the legal position of leaseholders may evolve further.

It is to be hoped that the present trend to longer leases will continue; if 999-year leases become general practice, leasehold extension will cease to be an issue. It is also reasonable to hope that some questionable practices by freeholders will either be legislated against or will die out: for instance, the writing into leases of sweeping and possibly unenforceable restrictions on leaseholders (see Chapter Two).

But there have been influential calls for more fundamental change. As was explained in Chapter One, 'freehold' and 'leasehold' property are concepts based on a way of thinking about land that, in its fundamentals, is unchanged since mediaeval times. So it is certainly arguable that this way of thinking is not suited to the widespread use of flats in modern housing. 'Commonhold' is a concept designed to sweep away ancient legal forms and replace them, so far as flats are concerned, with an entirely new form of tenure.

The new commonhold tenure has obvious attractions. An important one is that, in contrast to leasehold, ownership of the flats is not time limited; consequently there is no need for lease extension. But, in other respects, it is hard to see how a block owned on commonhold will differ greatly from one where the leaseholders have collectively enfranchised under the 1993 Act. And even the rule that leases must have a time limit is not necessarily as restrictive as it sounds, because it is not uncommon for leases to be granted for 999 years (occasionally even longer) which is effectively 'for ever' because the buildings to which they relate will almost certainly have ceased to exist long before the Thirtieth Century when the leases theoretically expire.

The underlying assumption behind commonhold is this: that the problem with leasehold tenure is that the interests of the freeholder on one hand, and the individual leaseholders on the other, are different because they are held by different people and it is this that causes so much conflict and dissatisfaction. If this assumption is correct, it is reasonable to believe that commonhold, by ensuring that the two different interests are held by the same people, will prove a more satisfactory type of tenure. It certainly seems to be on this basis that the Commonhold and Leasehold Reform Act 2002 was written; remarkably, it contains very little about disputes between the commonhold association and individual unit holders, presumably because it is thought that such disputes will seldom occur. Although there is some recognition in the draft regulations being consulted on at the time of writing (January 2003) that disputes will occur, it still seems to be assumed that they will be very rare and no attempt is made to give the commonhold association effective remedies if unit holders are in default.

It is respectfully suggested here that this is far too sanguine an assumption. The fundamental cause of conflict between leaseholders and freeholders is not that the interests are held by different people; it is that the interests themselves are unavoidably different. Simply put, what is in the interests of individual flats is not necessarily in the interests of the block as a whole, and individual leaseholders will always be reluctant to pay for things that bring them little or no benefit.

For instance, suppose the roof of a block of flats has begun to leak. This is disrepair concerning the fabric of the building so it is the responsibility of the freeholder or, in a commonhold block, the commonhold association. But if the leak is not yet very severe, only the owners of upper flats are likely to notice its effects and only they are likely to be strongly motivated to do anything about it. Other residents may well be inclined to put it off, particularly if the repair is costly.

In the real world of managing and maintaining blocks of flats this kind of conflict of interest arises all the time; commonhold status does nothing to resolve it. Moreover, commonhold associations, which will mostly be fairly small bodies without strong resources behind them, will face the same problems as are common to all organisations that rely on voluntary effort. Anyone that has been involved in a voluntary body will recognise the symptoms: often there is great initial enthusiasm but as time wears on people are less and less willing to give up their time to attend meetings and carry out essential administration.

Some of these comments also apply to the concept of a 'flying freehold'. This is an idea that has been mooted from time to time, again with the idea of doing away with leasehold as a way of owning flats. The reasoning is that the traditional concept of 'freehold' is essentially two-dimensional: the freehold relates to a defined patch of land that could be drawn on a map. In theory, it extends in one direction to the centre of the earth and in the other indefinitely upwards. The idea of a flying freehold is that the concept should be made *three*-dimensional, so that it would be possible not only, as now, to buy a piece of land on which a building happens to stand (see Chapter One), but also a defined volume of space, perhaps high above ground, that happens to contain a flat.

87

But, like commonhold, this pleasantly surreal idea does not really solve the fundamental problem in flats, which arises not from the legal technicalities of tenure but from the inescapable problem that there are two fundamentally different interests involved. The flat owners have responsibility for their own flats, but there has to be someone or something else that looks after the building as a whole; and this requires the spending of money, which in turn can come only from the flat owners. This awkward fact will have to allowed for by any new form of tenure, just as it is by the existing law of freeholder and leaseholder which, whatever its weaknesses and oddities, has shown that it can adapt to changing circumstances and has undeniably stood the test of time.

GLOSSARY

The purpose of this glossary is to explain some of the terms that are used in connection with leasehold property and may be unclear to users of this book (although for the sake of completeness one or two obvious words like 'rent' are included). It is not intended to give a precise legal definition, for which reference should be made to appropriate legal textbooks.

Assignment The transfer of a lease or tenancy from one person to another, usually by sale.

Blanket condition A term in a lease or tenancy that, if taken literally, would impose unreasonable constraints on the use of the premises.

Commonhold A new form of tenure introduced by the Commonhold and Leasehold Reform Act 2002. Owners of individual flats in a block all become members of the commonhold association, which owns the freehold of the block and manages and maintains it on their behalf.

Conveyance The transfer of a freehold from one person to another, usually by sale.

Determination A lease or tenancy is said to be determined when it is brought to an end by a positive act by either the landlord (freeholder) or tenant (leaseholder), as opposed to coming to an end because its term has expired. An outstanding example of a word used in one way by lawyers and another by everyone else.

Enfranchisement (individual) A lease is enfranchised when the leaseholder acquires the freehold. This has the effect of ending the lease and leaving the former leaseholder in sole possession of the freehold.

Enfranchisement (collective) The acquisition of the freehold on behalf of a number of leaseholders acting together.

Exclusive possession The right of a leaseholder or tenant to exclude other people, especially the landlord or freeholder, from the property.

Extension A lease is said to be extended when a longer term is agreed by both parties or (more usually) when it is replaced by a fresh lease with longer to run. The latter can happen either by agreement or as a result of the leaseholder exercising legal rights.

Fixed term A fixed term tenancy or lease is one with a defined ending date, as opposed to a periodic tenancy.

Forfeiture The ultimate penalty if the leaseholder has breached the terms of the lease: the courts can end it and return the property to the freeholder.

Freeholder The owner of the strongest title to land available under English law. Freehold is tantamount to outright ownership and is treated as such in this book. The term 'freeholder' is used throughout to refer to the person granting the lease, although this will not always be the case in practice in practice - see the section on *Head leases and subleases* in Chapter One.

Ground Rent A usually notional payment required under a lease, a source of income to the freeholder and a reminder to the leaseholder that he does not own the property outright.

Head lease When a leaseholder grants one or more subleases, the original lease is called the head lease.

Landlord The granter of a lease, tenancy, or licence.

Lease Strictly, the terms lease and tenancy are interchangeable. In this book, a lease is a tenancy with a fixed term of over seven years.

Leaseholder In this book, a tenant for a fixed term exceeding seven years.

Leasehold valuation tribunal A special committee appointed to settle disputes between freeholders and leaseholders arising from the entranchisement or extension of leases under the 1967, 1987, and 1993 Acts.

Licence Permission to occupy land not amounting to a tenancy or lease, usually because exclusive possession is not granted.

Long lease Defined for various purposes under the 1967, 1987, and 1993 Acts as a lease originally granted for a fixed term of over 21 years.

Low rent A level of rent defined in the 1967, 1987, and 1993 Acts in ways that are intended to exclude the rent likely to be paid under a periodic tenancy or short fixed term tenancy.

Managing agent An organisation or (seldom) individual appointed by a freeholder to carry out some or all of his management responsibilities.

Management agreement Legal contract appointing a managing agent.

Management fee Payment due from the freeholder to the managing agent.

Marriage value Value by which the elements brought together by a lease enfranchisement, or extension, exceed their combined value as separate entities before it took place. The marriage value is sometimes a component in calculating the premium when leases are extended or enfranchised.

Mixed tenure A mixed tenure block is one that contains both leasehold and tenanted property.

Mortgagee The person or (usually) financial institution lending money against the security of property. Not to be confused with the following.

Mortgagor The owner of property, using it as security to raise a loan. 'Mortgagee' and 'mortgagor' are often confused, but if it is remembered that the owner of the property can be said to have mortgaged it, the difference becomes clear.

Nominee purchaser Whoever is chosen by the leaseholders involved in collective enfranchisement to be the new owner of the freehold: usually a company they have set up for the purpose.

Onerous condition A term in a lease or tenancy that seriously affects its market value.

Open market value The value of any saleable item assuming a willing seller and a willing buyer. The open market value of a freehold or a lease is a component in calculating the premium when leases are extended or enfranchised.

Peppercorn A notional rent is often called a peppercorn - an unusually fanciful piece of legal jargon..

Period of grace Leases sold under the right to buy, and occasionally other leases, contain an estimate of future service charges, usually for the first five years of the lease. During this 'period of grace' any spending above the estimate cannot be recovered.

Periodic A periodic tenancy is one that runs from period to period (usually week to week or month to month) until something intervenes to stop it: the opposite of a fixed term tenancy.

Pre-charging Charging for services in advance: used to build up a sinking fund.

Premium The payment due by the leaseholder to the freeholder when a lease is enfranchised or extended.

Qualifying leaseholders (or qualifying tenants) The tenants or leaseholders that qualify for the various rights, under the 1967, 1987, or 1993 Acts, to enfranchise or extend leases. The qualifications vary depending which right is being exercised under which Act.

Quiet enjoyment The right of leaseholders and tenants not to have their use of the property interfered with by the landlord: closely allied to exclusive possession.

Recognised tenants' association Body of leaseholders and/or tenants recognised by the freeholder for consultation purposes.

Re-entry Regaining possession of a property, for instance at the end of a tenancy or lease.

Rent Payment of (almost always) money in exchange for being allowed to occupy property under a lease, tenancy, or licence.

Residence test Requirement for most purposes under the 1967, 1987, and 1993 Acts that a leaseholder must live on the premises, or have done so in the recent past. The exact test varies depending which right is being exercised.

Reversioner The person to whom possession will revert when the existing lease or tenancy comes to an end; usually the freeholder.

Right to buy A scheme, originally under the Housing Act 1980, allowing tenants of local authorities and some housing associations to buy their homes at a substantial discount.

Service charge Payment by leaseholders and tenants for services provided by the freeholder.

Shared ownership A scheme for assisted house purchase on part-buy, part-rent terms.

Sinking fund A fund built up on the service charge account by pre-charging.

Staircasing The purchase by a shared owner of an additional share of the property.

Sublease A lease granted by a leaseholder.

Tenant For the purpose of this book, someone holding a periodic tenancy or a tenancy granted for a fixed term of less than seven years.

Term The time for which a lease or fixed term tenancy will run.